OPENING
THE DOOR

DEVELOPED BY
RON BENNETT & LARRY GLABE

OPENING
THE DOOR

DEVELOPED BY
RON BENNETT & LARRY GLABE

NAVPRESS

BRINGING TRUTH TO LIFE
P.O. Box 35001, Colorado Springs, Colorado 80935

The Navigators is an international Christian organization. Our mission is to reach, disciple, and equip people to know Christ and to make Him known through successive generations. We envision multitudes of diverse people in the United States and every other nation who have a passionate love for Christ, live a lifestyle of sharing Christ's love, and multiply spiritual laborers among those without Christ.

NavPress is the publishing ministry of The Navigators. NavPress publications help believers learn biblical truth and apply what they learn to their lives and ministries. Our mission is to stimulate spiritual formation among our readers.

The Navigators Church Discipleship Ministry (CDM) is focused on helping churches become more intentional in disciple making. CDM staff nationwide are available to help church leadership develop the critical components that will enable them to accomplish Christ's Great Commission. For further information on how CDM can help you, contact our office at 719-594-2446.

Copyright © The Navigators Church Discipleship Ministries
All rights reserved. No part of this publication may be reproduced (except where noted) in any form without written permission from The Navigators, Church Discipleship Ministries, P.O. Box 6000, Colorado Springs, CO 80934. ISBN 1-57683-346-1

Cover Design: Kristi Walling
Cover Illustration: DigitalVision
Creative Team: Paul Santhouse, Melissa Munro, Greg Clouse, Glynese Northam

Some of the anecdotal illustrations in this book are true to life and are included with the permission of the persons involved. All other illustrations are composites of real situations, and any resemblance to people living or dead is coincidental.

Unless otherwise identified, all Scripture quotations in this publication are taken from the HOLY BIBLE: NEW INTERNATIONAL VERSION® (NIV®). Copyright © 1973, 1978, 1984 by International Bible Society. Used by permission of Zondervan Publishing House. All rights reserved. Other versions used include: *The New Testament in Modern English* (PH), J. B. Phillips, Translator, © J. B. Phillips, 1958, 1960, 1972, used by permission of Macmillan Publishing Company.

Printed in the United States of America
1 2 3 4 5 6 7 8 9 10 / 06 05 04 03 02

FOR A FREE CATALOG OF
NAVPRESS BOOKS & BIBLE STUDIES,
CALL 1-800-366-7788 (USA)
OR 1-416-499-4615 (CANADA)

For further information regarding this material and other discipling resources contact:

The Navigators
P.O. Box 6000
Colorado Springs, CO 80934

TABLE OF CONTENTS

PREFACE 7

THE CHALLENGE 9
    Wanted: Mountain Climber 9
    Reaching People Where They Are 12
    Learning Through Illustration.................13
    The Final Challenge.................................14

LEADER'S GUIDE 15
    Using the Discovery Guides 15
    Planning...17
    Preparation 20
    Facilitating 21
    Recruiting 23
    Sharing Salvation 25

LEADER PREPARATION MATERIALS 29

DISCOVERY GUIDES..................................33

APPENDIX 97
    A. Basic Laws of Spiritual Economics.....97
    B. Spiritual Journey 98
    C. Bridge Illustration 99

PREFACE

For most people the thought of doing evangelism produces the same emotional reaction as imagining a two-year-old running loose in a china shop—fear, anxiety, an instant aerobic heart rate, sweaty palms, and frantic glances for the exit signs.

Evangelism-induced anxiety (EIA syndrome) can result from several things. Like the parent of a toddler in a china shop, most fear a disaster as mild as embarrassment or as extensive as bankruptcy.

Many excellent books exist on the subject of evangelism. It would be redundant, if not presumptuous on my part, to add to the list. My purpose is simply to reduce the EIA syndrome by providing a user- and receiver-friendly tool.

I am not an evangelist. My desire to reach the lost comes from my own personal relationship with Christ and my understanding of Christ's Great Commission. I have learned by observation, practice, mistakes, failures, and more practice. I've adapted, experimented, and persisted. Out of this journey of discovery, I developed this material.

I have also learned that to mobilize the body of Christ to reach our world, evangelism cannot rely on the professional or the gifted. We must understand that evangelism is a process and not simply an event. Everyone, regardless of gifting, can contribute.

That process is part of everyone's spiritual journey and involves sowing, cultivating, and harvesting. For some, the journey is short and straight. For others, it is long and serpentine.

Evangelism recognizes these stages and seeks to deliberately contribute to the process. Each phase requires different strategies. For those who choose to be part of a planned, strategic outreach, developing proper skills and tools for each stage becomes critical.

In order to find the appropriate tools, we must understand that there are basically three responses to the gospel:
1. "I'm not interested—get lost,"
2. "I understand—help me," and
3. "I'm not convinced—but interested."

Paul, the great evangelist, received the same responses in his address to the crowd on Mars Hill in Athens.

When they heard about the resurrection of the dead, some of them sneered, but others said, "We want to hear you again on this subject.". . . A few men became followers of Paul and believed. (Acts 17:32-34, emphasis added)

The first two responses are the easiest to deal with: "Get lost" and "Help me." However, most people are in the last category—curious but not convinced. So what tools can we use to share the gospel with them?

Harvesting tools, those that summarize the gospel and bring people to a point of decision, are the most familiar. Tracts like *Peace with God, The Four Spiritual Laws,* or summary illustrations like *The Bridge* are designed to harvest what is mature. The purpose of these tools is to draw a line in the sand, to test to see if the harvest is ripe, to encourage a decision. Yet in the process of coming to Christ, many people are still in the cultivation stage: exploring, seeking, asking, wrestling. They need understanding—not a line drawn in the sand prematurely.

We need a tool that exposes seekers to the reality of Christ in the Scriptures so their faith can grow. "Faith comes from hearing the message, and the message is heard through the word of Christ" (Romans 10:17).

Opening the Door is a cultivation tool that will progressively help people discover and understand the gospel of Jesus Christ.

Opening the Door will help a person answer four critical life questions:
1. Who is Jesus Christ?
2. What does He say about putting life together?
3. What are the implications for me?
4. How will I respond?

No tool is effective by itself. There is no substitute for prayer and the work of the Holy Spirit. My hope is that *Opening the Door* will fit as one quality tool in your expanding ministry toolbox and help you overcome EIA syndrome.

THE CHALLENGE

There is a growing concern that the church today is strategically poised for a ministry of irrelevance. A polar drift is occurring putting distance between our society and the church.

The scene in America is like a culture lost in the mountains while the church is operating in the valley. Strategies and tactics effective in the past are now becoming increasingly irrelevant and ineffective in today's mountain culture. If Christians are going to be salt and light in this decade, we need to undergo a radical change in vision, values, and lifestyles.

> **Classified**
> **WANTED:** Mountain climbers to join expedition for search and rescue operations in the highlands of America. Training provided.

The need of the hour is for a band of mountain climbers conditioned and equipped to climb in the mountains of our society. Their mission is not survival, photography, or recreation. Instead, their mission is to search and rescue the sur-vivors trapped in the avalanches of sin, self, and secularism.

Caleb was an Old Testament climber, a real mountain man. Moses originally sent him and eleven others to survey the Promised Land. He and Joshua gave the minority opinion on the feasibility of possessing this land. The majority opinion broke faith in God. They viewed the giants and walled cities as insurmountable considering their own resources. God's judgment on that generation was to hold them to their decision. For the next forty years they roamed in the desert. God gave the privilege of entering the Promised Land to the next generation.

However, as a result of Caleb's faithful service, Moses gave a promise. Caleb's inheritance would be the land he viewed on that original mission.

When Joshua began to allot the new land to the various family tribes, Caleb asked for the high country, the mountains of Hebron, which included the walled cities and giants he had witnessed forty-five years earlier. It was tough terrain, the hard job, the job yet unfinished. Unlike other tribes of Israel who settled for the easy land east of the Jordan, Caleb went for the mountains.

What qualities made Caleb a real mountain man? First, he was **Confident in the Promises of God**. "Now give me this hill country that the LORD promised me that day" (Joshua 14:12). Caleb believed God's promise made decades earlier (Joshua 14:9). Time had not diminished the validity of God's word. The basis for requesting his inheritance was not his own merit but the promise of God.

Caleb was also **Content in the Providence of God**. "Now then, just as the LORD promised, he has kept me alive for forty-five years" (Joshua 14:10). Thankfulness in God's sovereign goodness was still his attitude at age eighty-five. He could have reflected on the injustice of spending forty years living in a sand pile with a bunch of losers. He could have been bitter over being penalized for the mistakes of others. He could have easily considered the best years of his life wasted . . . for doing right!

Yet Caleb's view of God's providence was one of humble acceptance. He simply accepted the cards God dealt him with gratitude and humility. Content in the providence of God, Caleb seized the moment of opportunity.

Too often, resentment over circumstances blinds us to the opportunities of the moment. Chained to the past through attitudes of ungratefulness and resentment, we fail to see what God is doing in the present. These attitudes deplete our emotional energy. We become weary and confused. Contentment with God's sovereignty made Caleb like the Energizer bunny. He just kept going and going and going.

In addition, Caleb was also **Competent in the Presence of God**. "Now give me this hill country . . . and their cities . . . large and fortified . . . the LORD helping me, I will drive them out just as he said" (Joshua 14:12).

No illusions of grandeur here. Oh yes, he was still an eager and wiry warrior. However, his strength was not the basis for success. Caleb knew that he could be victorious only if Yahweh went with him. Maybe it was the model of Moses that left this principle indelibly etched on his mind. "If you do not go with us," Moses had said to God, "then do not lead us out from this place" (see Exodus 33:15).

Caleb was not referring to God's omnipresence. Caleb was dependent on the experiential, personal presence of God that results from union with Him.

No mountain venture, no matter how commendable, can succeed without the presence and power of God. The dangers are too real, our resources too inadequate, the job too big. To climb in the rugged mountains of our society, we need to find our competence in His presence and power.

Caleb was a person with the faith and courage to take on the tough job. Highlighted in biblical history, he was one who made a difference in his generation.

This generation also needs Calebs, people who have the vision and courage to take on the tough job of climbing into the mountains of our culture. God is still looking for people with a vision for the high country, people not paralyzed by circumstances or popular opinion.

We cannot remain in the valley and send messages to those stranded in the mountains. Get-well cards and road maps are inadequate for those trapped, starved, and without hope. Ski trips, nature tours, and photo sessions still leave lost people isolated, injured, and scared.

The need of this hour is for men and women to leave the comfort and security of the valley. Their mission: to climb into the mountains of our society to reach people who need Christ. Few lost people today will accidentally wander out of the mountains into the valley to find the help they need.

Those who would follow Jesus into the mountains in our day must be Calebs who are AUTHENTIC. When Jesus described what it meant to be His disciple, He used the word "tested" or "proven" disciple (John 15:8, PH). He was referring to a follower who was real. A follower of Jesus takes on Christ's nature and character. Discipleship is not a spiritual version of behavior modification. It is real life change . . . from the inside out.

Jesus said a trained disciple will become like his teacher. Followers of Christ who are in personal, dynamic union with Him are in the exciting process of inner change. They are more than "change agents"—they are "changed agents."

However, being authentic doesn't mean perfection. It does mean progress. It means to be proactive, not passive. It means that we are "working out" that which God has placed within (Philippians 2:12).

Authenticity is the spiritual prerequisite for mountain climbing. No wise person would venture into the mountains if he were not in good physical shape. Union with Christ as a daily growing experience is the spiritual conditioning needed to survive in the mountains of our culture.

Today's mountain climbers also must develop INTEGRATED lives. God desires to integrate kingdom living into every facet of life. Jesus never separated life into the sacred and secular. Climbers cannot survive in the mountains with a compartmentalized, segmented approach to life. The kingdom of God lays claim to every aspect of life. Living by the values and principles of the kingdom is not simply a creed; it is a lifestyle.

Scripture is God's manual for integrated living. The Scripture is more than sermon material for pastors. It is the practical handbook for every generation and every individual who claims to be a follower of Christ. "The Scriptures are the comprehensive equipment of the man of God, and fit him fully for all branches of his work" (2 Timothy 3:17, PH). It sounds strangely hollow when a person claims to follow Christ and yet fails to practice (or even know) what God says about conducting the affairs of life.

Today's spiritual mountain climbers are also **CONNECTED**. No one survives the hazards of the mountains alone. One of Satan's favorite strategies is to isolate us from the support of the body. Search and rescue teams tie themselves together for support, encouragement, and protection. "Two are better than one. . . . If one falls down, his friend can help him up.

But pity the man who falls and has no one to help him up!" (Ecclesiastes 4:9-10).

Being connected means more than casual fellowship at church on Sunday morning. It means regular personal accountability and encouragement with fellow climbers. Climbers work together with those of like heart and vision. Committed to each other and the mission, climbers form a working unit. They experience the dynamics of unity while focused on a specialized task. Each person, as part of the team, brings to the whole his or her gifts and strengths.

Climbing teams are needed. The easy job has been done. Reaching those who live in the valley has largely been accomplished. It is the mountain country that remains to be possessed. God is looking for the Calebs of this generation who will leave the security and comfort of the valley and venture into the mountains.

REACHING PEOPLE WHERE THEY ARE

Jesus excelled at going into the mountains. One of His outstanding characteristics was that He went where people were. He chose to encounter diverse people in diverse situations. At home, the marketplace, the temple, a meadow, a lake . . . all were strategic to Jesus. He had the knack (or strategy?) of meeting people on their turf—where they were comfortable.

The gospel records show that wher-

ever Jesus went He drew a crowd. So magnetic was Jesus that people, having met Him, brought others for a firsthand look. Philip found Nathaniel and said, "We have found the one Moses wrote about. . . . Come and see" (John 1:45-46). A Samaritan woman, having encountered Jesus at the local watering hole, returned to her relational network and said, "Come, see a man who told me everything I ever did" (John 4:29).

With various motives, they came. They listened. They watched. Some touched. Some wondered. But having come, no one left the same. No one who encountered Jesus could ever be neutral.

In a society drifting in a sea of relativity and the fog of humanism, we need to introduce people to the One who came as the Author and Restorer of Life. Too often we have subtly and erroneously focused on presenting church, religion, ourselves . . . rather than Jesus.

In a society that increasingly regards the institutional church as irrelevant at best, we need a new strategy and new tools for reaching those in the mountains. Since many are now a second and third generation outside the church environ-ment, we need to recognize their shifting worldview and lack of biblical knowledge. We need a strategy that brings people into contact with the Jesus of the Bible, one that allows Jesus to meet them where they are, on their turf.

Opening the Door is a Bible discussion guide that enables those who are seeking truth for their lives to take a firsthand look at the records regarding Jesus. This guide helps people get to know Jesus "up close and personal," exposing many to Scripture for the first time. It enables people who are seekers to look at Jesus without first becoming skilled in religious tradition and knowledge. The questions in each Discovery Guide will help people better understand what Jesus did, said, and implied.

LEARNING THROUGH ILLUSTRATION

To reach those in the "mountains" of our society, we need to understand that most adults learn best through self-discovery. Most of us react negatively to being told what truth is. We want to discover truth for ourselves. Many adults also resist a fill-in-the-blank approach to discovering biblical truth. They suspect having views forced on them. What many need is the opportunity to look at the biblical records, discover, understand, and come to their own convictions. Our role is to create the opportunity for guided self-discovery.

Opening the Door studies a series of incidents in the life of Jesus where He demonstrates and teaches truth. In that original setting, people had to deal with His claims. They reacted as people do today. To a seeker, these reactions help them identify their own journey.

The gospels, especially Luke and John, were written as either evangelism letters or letters for following up with new converts.

Therefore, since I myself have carefully investigated everything from the beginning, it seemed good also to me to write an orderly account for you, most excellent Theophilus, so that you may know the certainty of the things you have been taught. (Luke 1:3-4)

Jesus did many other miraculous signs in the presence of his disciples, which are not recorded in this book. But these are written that you may believe that Jesus is the Christ, the Son of God, and that by believing you may have life in his name. (John 20:30-31)

Opening the Door reveals the facts surrounding a particular incident found in the text. Additional background information is given for each incident where it may prove helpful in understanding the story. Key words are also defined so that no outside reference or prior knowledge is required.

Some of the questions lead a person to read between the lines where there is no right or wrong answer. Each person can then subjectively enter the story, allowing discussion regardless of his or her Scripture knowledge.

THE FINAL CHALLENGE

We need tools such as these to be equipped to climb the mountains and close the distance between our society and the church. We cannot remain in the valley and send messages to those stranded in the mountains. We must reach out to them and lead them through the process of discovering faith in Jesus Christ.

LEADER'S GUIDE

USING THE DISCOVERY GUIDES

The Discovery Guides beginning on page 33 are arranged in a simple, user-friendly format. Each page contains a scriptural passage along with questions and pertinent data. No Bible is required. This becomes a great equalizer for those with little Bible background.

Each passage is designed for one session of exploration. The seeker does not need to prepare in advance. You will photocopy the appropriate Discovery Guide for all those involved at each meeting. Both leader and seeker fill out the sheet as the discussion progresses. This format does not require you to have a hidden set of questions that must be remembered or written out covertly.

It is important to keep the original Discovery Guide clean for future use with others. Each time you lead a Discovery group, start with a clean copy of the Discovery Guide. Each person's discovery process will be unique.

Opening the Door is built around eight key questions. They are the same for each passage discussed. These questions allow the participants to explore the passage at their own level of understanding. They are designed to take the participants from a cursory discovery of what the passage says to a more critical level of meaning and implication.

The key questions are:

1. **WHO** are the main characters in the story? Jesus will always be one. Other individuals or groups of people may be identified by name and/or by description. The main characters are those who interact with Jesus or are acted upon by Him.

2. **WHERE AND WHEN** does the action take place? Often the scene is described in terms of a location or setting. It is important to see that it was an actual event in real, space-time history. Certain stories will have more detail than others. Sometimes no information regarding time and location is given. However, developing a mental picture of the setting can aid in grasping the meaning of the passage.

3. **WHAT ARE THE KEY EVENTS, ACTIVITIES, OR IDEAS?** Discover the action and activities that take place as well as

the key ideas for each incident. This information is available directly from the text and encourages further discovery. It is important to discuss the events even if they seem obvious. Discussing the action or events of the story gets people focused and involved in the conversation.

4. **RESPONSE AND WHY?** This question asks the participants to identify the reactions of the main characters to what Jesus said and did. Sometimes the reaction is given in the text. Other times it can be surmised from the context. At other times, it must be speculated. WHY people reacted the way they did promotes critical discussion that allows people to enter the story in a subjective way.

5. **NAMES AND CLAIMS** made about Jesus? This question develops the understanding of who Jesus is. These names and claims can be stated or inferred. They can come from the main characters or Jesus Himself. Ultimately, the gospel writers recorded each story or incident to tell us something about Jesus. Understanding these claims is the heart and focus of these studies.

6. **VALUES?** Values are the ideas presented as having critical worth and importance. They may be stated or implied. Because a person's behavior is derived from a core set of values, Jesus taught and modeled the values necessary for successful living. For example, Jesus often highlights faith as a supreme value in His teaching.

7. **BELIEFS?** Beliefs are the concepts Jesus taught to be truth. They may be in the form of a principle or idea. Beliefs may deal with the spiritual or physical dimensions of life, or with character or conduct. Identifying the beliefs in the passage doesn't mean that those in the group need to personally buy into the belief.

8. **CONCLUSIONS AND IMPLICATIONS?** This question allows participants to summarize what they have learned or feel is critical. It allows them to highlight key discoveries and personalize the truth the Holy Spirit emphasizes. This does not mean that each person will believe all that has been discovered. He or she may understand that a passage is teaching a point and not believe it yet. This question leads to an "if . . . then" response. *If* this point is true . . . *then* what are the implications to life in general and to my life in particular?

This process of discovery allows the Holy Spirit to use His Word to penetrate the hearts of people in search of truth. Our responsibility is to expose people to truth and help bring understanding. Only God can open the hearts of people so that His truth becomes personal and effective.

PLANNING

Leading this study requires organization and planning. It involves knowing your audience and how to best meet their needs.

One-to-One or Small Groups

Opening the Door can be used either in a small group or one-on-one. Most Bible study discussions are difficult to lead in a one-on-one setting since the leader asks the questions and the other person fills in the response. However, this study allows mutual discovery as both persons explore the passage as fellow pilgrims and share what they discover.

Open groups

This format allows people to join a Discovery group after it is in progress. Although it is helpful to build a reservoir of understanding of what Jesus did and said, it is not essential for participating in a discussion. Nor is the sequence of the material in the gospel critical to understanding the truths. Each passage studied relates to a whole yet stands on its own. If a person misses a discussion or comes in later, he or she is not "behind." This ongoing format allows new people to visit or join at any time rather than waiting until a new group forms.

Frequency

The leader should set the frequency of discussions in keeping with his or her audience. For some, a weekly discussion is appropriate. For others, it may be monthly. Since no preparation is required on the part of the seeker, frequency is simply an issue of availability.

Normally seekers can absorb only a little exposure at a time. It is better to have short, lively, stimulating discussions than long, dead ones. The Discovery Guides format easily fits into an early morning breakfast, a lunch period, or an hour or so during the evening.

Teamwork

Working as a team is an asset in launching a Discovery group. One person leads the discussion; the others serve as hosts. Everyone can participate in the Discovery discussion. A team approach allows complementary gifts to be used in creating an attractive atmosphere.

In the marketplace, for example, a team of people can function well if all the participants work in the same vicinity. They each bring a seeker friend to the discussion over lunch or breakfast. One person facilitates the discussion while the others help develop an atmosphere of love and acceptance. It is important *not* to have more believers attend than seekers. The atmosphere changes when believers dominate. It can cease to be seeker friendly.

It is also critical that those believers who attend are sensitive to seekers and their process. The Discovery sessions are not to become preaching opportunities for favorite Christian issues. Christians must be sensitive to the fact that seekers may have a different worldview.

Your Home a Lighthouse by Bob and Betty Jacks (NavPress, 1986) offers good material on using a team approach, as does Bob and Matthew Jacks' *Divine Appointments* (NavPress, 2002).

Other resources and methods

The Discovery sessions also work well in conjunction with *The New 2:7 Series*.

As group members pray for a list of potential people in their networks that could be invited to a Discovery group, they prepare to lead by working through the material in *Opening the Door*.

Once people are familiar with the material and ready to launch their Discovery group, they (or a team) begin their own small group. The original group then acts as a ministry support group to encourage, pray, and provide resources. If groups of people in a local church lead Discovery groups, they could host periodic events for Discovery group members. For example, a dinner, barbecue, or sporting event could expose people to others in process. A credible speaker could share his or her testimony as a way of summarizing the gospel.

Location

Reaching the lost in today's society is an increasingly challenging mission. In the past some have found success in inviting seekers into a religious environment like the church. Though certain people may still respond to such an invitation, increasingly they are unwilling or unable to meet Christians on religious turf.

For those truly lost, it is a difficult request. They have neither the capacity for nor interest in valley functions. Our evangelistic tools tend to require more religious orientation than many people have. We are now dealing with people who have been trapped in the mountains for a second or even a third generation.

On neutral ground, both the leader and the seeker are comfortable. It is a place where both can feel safe. By reducing the environmental obstacles, we allow people to focus on the discovery process. If anyone is to be uncomfortable, it should be the Christian. A person with a mission (missionary) should adapt to the culture of those he or she is seeking to influence.

An office, a restaurant, or home are all potential neutral settings, depending on whom you are trying to reach. Many women feel very comfortable in each other's homes—especially if they are in the same general socioeconomic strata. Yet for some men, another person's home may make them uncomfortable. It is too intimate and personal. It may be too foreign to their experience or relational level.

Where you meet may also be influenced by when you meet. If it is early morning or over a lunch hour, the best place may be a conference room in the office or a restaurant close by.

Attendees

Begin to pray about those you know who might have an interest in looking at the life of Christ to discover what He has to say about Himself and how to live life. Making a list will assist you in consistent prayer. More help is included under Recruiting on page 23.

Content

As you consider possible invitees, you will need to reflect on where they are on their spiritual journey. Some will need more background than others. This study is designed to accommodate those with and without biblical background.

This study includes twenty-one passages selected from the life and ministry of Christ. Some deal with His claims and identity. Others deal with His teaching on life principles. Still others focus on the key elements of the gospel. You can include as many or as few as seems appropriate.

The chart on page 32 gives a list of the passages used in *Opening the Door*

and a summary of their content. Your own study of the passages will add to this summary overview. Each passage has a code letter to give you an idea of its focus:

I = Identity. Jesus is demonstrating His identity as God in the flesh.

L = Life Principles. Jesus is teaching how to live life with kingdom values, beliefs, and behavior.

G = Gospel. Jesus is dealing with core issues regarding His role as Savior.

I/G = Identity and Gospel. Jesus identifies Himself around a core gospel issue.

Each time you lead a Discovery series, the number of sessions may vary. Once you are comfortable with the material, you will be able to adapt your passages easily to your audience. Remember that the seeker is not looking for a survey of the Bible or even a Bible book. Therefore, it is not essential that you take the passages in any particular order. You could use any of the following options:

OPTION A: A five-session Discovery series
1. Luke 4:14-30 (I)
2. Luke 5:17-26 (I/G)
3. Luke 23:33-47 (G)
4. Luke 24:1-12 (G)
5. A summary presentation using the Bridge Illustration

OPTION B: A seven-session Discovery series

1. Luke 5:17-26 (I/G)
2. Luke 7:36-50 (I/G)
3. Luke 6:20-49 (L)
4. Luke 12:15-34 (L)
5. Luke 23:32-47 (G)
6. John 3:1-16 (G)
7. Summary presentation using the Bridge Illustration

OPTION C: An open-ended series where you continue as long as people remain interested.

In this type of series, you can proceed slower and cover more passages. If new people join your group, you may want to cycle back through the major truths using different passage selections.

The purpose of this style of Bible discussion is to help seekers understand truth. You will need to keep your audience in focus since this is not intended to be an in-depth study that would appeal to Christians. This study is designed to build truth upon truth—little by little. Seekers usually cannot take a great deal of content at one time. Constant exposure over a period of time allows the Holy Spirit to build line upon line. Don't be concerned if only a few truths are understood from a passage. Don't expect the seeker to see all that there is in a passage. Your contribution should add some to what he or she discovers but not too much. You are not primarily a teacher but a fellow traveler.

PREPARATION

As a leader, you need to personally study the passages before you lead a discussion with seekers. Such study does not need to be extensive but sufficient to become familiar with the passage. As you become familiar with the text, you will be able to guide others in discovery without dominating or manipulating the discussion. Your study will also give you a reservoir of insight from which to draw. It doesn't mean that you need to share *all* your insights. In fact, you should anticipate that the seeker will make observations and offer insights that are new to you. Indeed, without a church background, seekers will often see things that are refreshing and challenging.

Study forms are included for your use in the Leader Preparation Materials section, beginning on page 29. These guides are tools for purposeful verse-by-verse meditation. The passage may be familiar, but allow the Holy Spirit to give new insight—especially regarding values and principles. The sample form on page 30 gives some initial meditation on Luke 4:1-13. Remember always to leave your preparation for the study at home. As the leader, bring a clean copy of the Discovery Guide for everyone in the group—including yourself. This allows each member of the group to discover together. No two discussions are the same, even though the same passage is used.

Notes that you take during a discussion can be added to your study preparation material, as can new insights and questions that came up during your conversation. These items will help you be more prepared in the future.

FACILITATING

Leading a discussion using *Opening the Door* is really a matter of guiding or facilitating. Each of the eight questions in a session stimulates discovery and discussion. The benefit of the questions can vary with the passage, group, or individual. As you become more confident in guiding the discussion, you will discover greater freedom in using the questions and adding your own. The questions are meant to serve and not confine the leader.

Begin by reading the passage or having others read who you know are able and willing. It is not necessary to begin or end this discussion with prayer. Praying with a seeker can create an environment where he or she feels more like an outsider than a fellow participant.

Launch the first question by saying something like, *"Let's identify the main characters in the story and highlight what we know about them."* Stick primarily to what the passage itself reveals. If it doesn't say much, that's OK.

After identifying this general information, a subsequent question could be, *"What can we learn about where this story takes place? What is the setting—surroundings?" "What do you picture it would be like?"* (Background and key words may be helpful at this time.) In some passages it may also be helpful to trace the events of the story. These should be fairly obvious, allowing even the most reserved person to make some observations and gain confidence before approaching the more difficult questions.

Referring to the identified main characters, question how each reacted in the story. *"Was their reaction predictable? Why do you think they acted as they did? How would you have reacted if you had been at the scene?"*

This question gives some room to speculate beyond the text. It allows people to enter the story subjectively. They may feel safer, for example, pointing out that the crowd suspected Jesus rather than saying that's how they feel.

The next question might be, *"Usually in these incidents with Jesus, He makes some claims about Himself or others make claims about Him. Let's discover what they are in this story. What are the people in these paragraphs saying or thinking about Jesus? What do you feel you would be thinking if you had been there?"*

Having explored the more obvious aspects of the passage, next bring out the important transcendent truths. Ask, *"What are the values that you see Jesus demonstrating or teaching?"* Initially you may need to give an example of what you mean by values. (See page 30.) Your example may come from the passage or from life in general. Some of the values are obvious from what Jesus taught. Others are subtler, inferred by how Jesus acted and related.

The next question in the Discovery Guide deals with the truths or principles that Jesus taught or demonstrated. It is not important to differentiate between these two. They simply bring out the key truths of the passage from different angles.

For example, in the passage of the Good Samaritan (Luke 10:25-37), love is a key value. It is unimportant whether it surfaces in your discussion as a principle, truth, or value. It is only important that it is observed and discussed. The questions are designed to look at the passage from various angles in order to discover its meaning. Use them with freedom and flexibility, not rigidity.

The final question should give your group the chance to summarize what they have heard and stimulate personal reflection. You could ask, *"What are the implications of these key truths to our lives today? How would our office, neighborhood, or society look if we followed these truths? If, for example, we believed that love as demon-*

strated by the Good Samaritan was a critical value, how would it affect our lives?"

Don't force personal application. It is typically easier to talk in generalities than in specifics. You can count on the fact that each person in your group will be wrestling with the truth personally even though it is being discussed generally. And God will be using the truth of the Scripture in lives even if actual learning isn't always verbalized. One of the values of the story form is that it heightens retention. The more of a mental picture each person develops during the discussion, the easier it will be to recall and reflect. It becomes a mental hat rack on which to hang the key truths that emerge.

Conclude your discussion by giving a preview of the next discussion. A statement to arouse curiosity and interest will help create a sense of anticipation.

The Discovery Guides are designed to enable people to take notes. As the leader, your model will be contagious. As you write down key observations, others will follow. Taking notes, however, is not essential. Some may initially be more comfortable just listening. Some people are more wired to write. Don't force those who aren't. Let each do what is individually most comfortable. Remember that seekers are not interested in doing Bible study. The advantage of having the handout is that each person can take it along afterward regardless of whether he or she has taken notes or not. The Scripture passage is readily available without having to find it again in a Bible he or she may or may not have.

Remember these key points as you facilitate the discussion:

- **Give people time to look and share.** The passage may be unfamiliar. They may be slow readers. They may be insecure sharing in a group or even out loud. Initially, people may not understand what you are looking for as you ask the questions. The advantage of using similar questions for each session is that people learn what to look for. They will gain confidence with each new discussion.

- **Don't dominate the sharing.** Model what you are looking for without giving all the answers or taking away the more obvious ones. It is more important that a seeker discovers and shares the answer than it is to have the leader share it. People will come unglued with motivation as they discover truth for themselves. The more success a person has, the greater the participation.

- **Be content not to exhaust all the truths in the passage.** You may have many observations that you don't share. Ensure that key concepts surface, but don't worry about being comprehensive. The goal is not to impress others with your knowledge or over-

whelm them with truth. God will use a little bit of truth in a big way. Too much new information can cause seekers to retreat. Be sensitive to what the Spirit of God is doing and stay in step. Get excited about what others discover.

RECRUITING

Recruiting is the process of enlisting others to join a group or a cause. A motorist whose car is stuck recruits those passing by to help him push it out. An organization recruits volunteers to assist at the annual blood drive. The PTA recruits parents to help with school functions.

These examples of recruiting are viewed positively by our society for two reasons. One, the people have been offered a choice to participate rather than being coerced. Two, the people find some satisfaction in the accomplishment of the task.

The stereotype of a car salesman, on the other hand, is generally viewed as pressuring people into buying a car they don't want, with money they don't have, at a price that's too high! Society views this type of "recruiting" as negative because of unfair pressure.

Unfortunately, this negative stereotype has discouraged us from recruiting seekers to investigate the claims of Christ. We find ourselves questioning the value of what we have to offer. We may wonder if they really need to have it. Are we benefiting them or just intruding into their lives?

Recruiting involves more than simply making information available. A person washed overboard needs more than the knowledge that a life preserver is onboard ship. She needs someone who will get the life preserver into her grasp.

Scripture makes it clear that every person has a spiritual dimension to his or her life. When Jesus encountered people, He saw more than their outward appearance. He also saw their spiritual condition. In Matthew 9 Jesus described people as distressed and downcast like sheep without a shepherd. In light of this observation, He was willing to offer the good news of the gospel to them. He recruited them to truth by taking the initiative graciously.

The following steps may be helpful in recruiting others for a Discovery group.

1. IDENTIFY. Identify those in your God-given networks you could invite to a Discovery session. Networks are relationships where you live, work, and play—those with whom you share some common ground or common interests. Then, decide who specifically God is putting on your heart to recruit. Write those names on a three-by-five-inch index card and pray for them daily.

2. INTRODUCE. Next, introduce the topic of spiritual issues with those on your prayer list. One way to bring up spiritual issues is to reflect on the four major dimensions of life: physical, spiritual, social, and intellectual. I tell people that I am interested in all four. Most people have given some thought to each one to some degree. I mention that I'd be interested in their thoughts on the spiritual dimension. I request their permission to ask questions that will give them a chance to relate what they think.

Any of the following questions would work:

- If you were to take a snapshot of your life ten years from now, what would it look like?
- What critical factors are necessary for you to feel successful?
- An author went around the country recently asking people, "What is the meaning of life?" If he were to ask you that question, how would you respond?
- What role does God play in your snapshot, critical factors, or view of the meaning of life?

My objective is not just to ask questions, but to open dialogue on a spiritual level. The more I have been able to discuss a variety of topics with a person, the easier and more natural it is to discuss spiritual topics.

3. **INVITE.** The next step is to invite people to investigate what Christ says about Himself and how to live life. You are not recruiting them to consider what the church says, or Christians say, or even what the Bible says. A seeker may view these opinions as irrelevant or incomprehensible. You want them to look at what Jesus says. And what He says happens to be recorded in a particular part of the Bible. Personally, I attempt to generate interest by telling them that Jesus has made some unique claims about Himself and how to live life.

You can then clearly and specifically ask if they would be interested in investigating what He has to say. It is critical to let each person answer. Often they will have questions or concerns about how this will take place. Address each concern honestly. As a person realizes that the Discovery group format is personal, practical, and relevant, he or she is more likely to try it.

4. **INFORM.** The last step is to inform them of the specifics. Tell them how long you will meet, where, who will attend, and so on. (Decide these logistics in advance.) Some will respond to an open-ended type format. Others will want to know that it has a fixed length with a clear beginning and end.

SHARING SALVATION

In the process of coming to Christ, each person has a history. God uses people and circumstances in each person's life to move that person closer to Himself. We need to be aware of and build upon that process. As we learn and value the person's journey, we communicate love and build a stronger bond of trust.

It was after many months of ministry and exposure that Jesus asked the disciples the critical question, "Who do you say that I am?" Today, as people discover the truth about Christ, they also need to be asked that same question. But we must start from their present position.

Spiritual Journey

One way to find out about a person's spiritual journey is to observe what he or she says over a period of time. Another way is to ask the person to describe it. You may say, "Bob, I make the assumption that everyone is on a spiritual journey. I'd be interested in hearing about yours. If you could graph it over time, what would it look like?"

He or she then can describe it verbally or use a graph to indicate the significant events, people, and impact. If you do this with a group, you can hand it out as an assignment for a future time or do it spontaneously. It is not surprising that once you ask a person about his or her spiritual journey, the person usually will ask you about yours.

Since each person's story is personal, it is imperative that it be shared in an atmosphere of trust. This very well may be a first-time experience. For some it is a risky exposure. They will ask, "If you know this about me, will you still accept me?" People will be more willing to share if they feel you sincerely want to know and value their story.

See the appendix for a copy of the Spiritual Journey illustration. You can photocopy this form and hand it out for people to share from when you feel it would be appropriate.

Summarizing

There are a variety of ways to summarize the gospel of Christ so that a person can make a faith response, including tracts such as *Peace with God* or *The Four Spiritual Laws*. Each of these gives a person a concise summary of the gospel with key questions to ask as you read through the presentation.

The Bridge to Life is another helpful evangelistic tool, one that allows you to draw a summary picture of the gospel. One significant benefit of The Bridge is that by memorizing the simple illustration, you can use it at any time. A copy of this illustration with a suggested presentation is included in the appendix. You also can purchase this in tract form

if you want to hand it out to your group.

It is highly recommended that you make a summary presentation of the gospel to each person in the Discovery group, either individually or as a group. An effective follow-up would be to meet individually with those from your group after they have attended three to five sessions. This also gives the leader a chance to see what the Holy Spirit is doing on a personal level. Often people are more transparent in a one-on-one situation than in a group.

A summary illustration is also a non-threatening way to help those who have not attended all the discussion sessions to get an overview of the gospel. You could say, "John, how about getting together for coffee next Thursday? I'd like to go over what we've been covering in our Discovery group. I can summarize the key issues and find out what you think about the discussions so far."

Another possible summary tool is the "Basic Laws of Spiritual Economics," included in the Appendix on page 97. It is specifically written to communicate to someone in the business world.

Helping seekers understand truth is essential for personal faith. Paul writes in 2 Corinthians 4:4 that Satan blinds the mind of the unbeliever. We are in a spiritual battle for the minds of men and women. Our arguments and logic are inadequate to release people's minds to truth. Exposure to His Word and prayer are our strong spiritual weapons against a powerful foe.

Opening the Door lends itself to this cultivation phase of evangelism. It allows discovery of truth without drawing a line in the sand. There obviously must be a place for commitment and decisions. But if we use a reaping method when the ground needs to be cultivated, we can alienate our audience. Remember, coming to Christ is a process. We want to move each person closer to Christ and a personal commitment of faith.

LEADER PREPARATION MATERIALS

The pages in this section may be photocopied as needed.

Text: _Luke 4:1-13_   Date: _____

Verse	What Happened	Response & Why	Names/Claims	Values	Beliefs
1	Returned from Jordan	Led by Spirit	Full of Holy Spirit		
2	Tempted 40 days	Ate nothing, hungry			Satan is real, enemy of God
3	Test: stones into bread		Son of God		
4		Quoted Scripture/direct		Life more than physical	
5	Showed kingdoms				
6	Test: worship Devil				
7					
8		Quoted Scripture/true		Worship God only	
9	Test: jump		Son of God		
10	Devil quotes Script.				
11					
12		Quotes Scripture/ authoritative			Scripture is authoritative and rule for life
13	Devil leaves				
			sample		

Conclusions/implications: _Satan is real. There is a spiritual battle going on between God and the Devil, a struggle that affects the welfare of man. Jesus didn't give in to Satan's temptations. He was always obedient to His Father's will. Jesus knew who He was (the Son of God) and didn't need to prove it to Satan. There is more to life than the physical. The spiritual is also real and ultimately the foundation for life._

Text: _____ Date: _____

Verse	What Happened	Response & Why	Names/Claims	Values	Beliefs

Conclusions/implications: _____

_____

_____

_____

_____

PASSAGE SUMMARY

Passage	Code	Description	Claims, Values, Beliefs
Luke 4:1-13	I	Jesus tempted by Satan	Reality of Satan, spiritual conflict
Luke 4:14-30	I	Jesus states His mission in home town	Prophecy fulfilled, compassion
Luke 4:31-44	I	Jesus' healing ministry	Power, authority, compassion
Luke 5:1-11	I	Jesus calls disciples to follow Him	Authority, knowledge, worthiness
Luke 5:17-26	I/G	Jesus heals paralytic	Authority to forgive, deity, faith
Luke 5:27-38	I	Jesus calls Levi to follow Him	Repentance, love for sinners
Luke 6:20-49	L	Jesus teaches on life principles	Heart problem, mercy, humility
Luke 7:1-10	I/G	Centurion's servant healed	Humility, faith, authority, hope
Luke 7:36-50	I/G	Immoral woman finds forgiveness	Compassion, grace, forgiveness
Luke 8:40-56	I/G	Jairus' daughter healed	Power, faith, peace
Luke 9:18-27	I	Disciples confess Christ's deity	Deity, life, death, resurrection
Luke 9:28-36	I	Christ's transfiguration	Jesus supersedes Law and Prophets God verifies Christ's identity
Luke 10:25-37	L	Parable of good Samaritan	Compassion, love, sacrifice
Luke 12:15-34	L	Rich and foolish man	Spiritual riches, God's care, real treasure, priority
Luke 14:15-34	G	Parable of the banquet	Kingdom invitation, must respond
Luke 15:11-32	I/G	Parable of prodigal son	Love, hope, forgiveness/repentance
Luke 17:20-35	G	Jesus predicts His return	Judgment, Christ returns
Luke 23:1-25	G	Pilate tries Jesus and finds innocent	Christ's innocence
Luke 23:32-47	G	Christ's crucifixion	Suffering, innocence, death
Luke 24:1-12	G	Resurrection of Jesus	Historic resurrection of Jesus
John 3:1-16	G	Jesus dialogues with Nicodemus	New birth, love, faith in Christ

Code Symbol

I   = Identity. Jesus is demonstrating His identity as God in the flesh.
L   = Life Principles. Jesus is teaching how to live life with kingdom values, beliefs, and behavior.
G   = Gospel. Jesus is dealing with core issues regarding His role as Savior.
I/G = Identity and Gospel. Jesus identifies Himself around a core gospel issue.

DISCOVERY GUIDES

The pages in this section may be photocopied as needed.

Luke 4:1-13

¹Jesus, full of the Holy Spirit, returned from the Jordan and was led by the Spirit in the desert, ²where for forty days he was tempted by the devil. He ate nothing during those days, and at the end of them he was hungry.

³The devil said to him, "If you are the Son of God, tell this stone to become bread."

⁴Jesus answered, "It is written: 'Man does not live on bread alone.'"

⁵The devil led him up to a high place and showed him in an instant all the kingdoms of the world. ⁶And he said to him, "I will give you all their authority and splendor, for it has been given to me, and I can give it to anyone I want to. ⁷So if you worship me, it will all be yours."

⁸Jesus answered, "It is written: 'Worship the LORD your God and serve him only.'"

⁹The devil led him to Jerusalem and had him stand on the highest point of the temple. "If you are the Son of God," he said, "throw yourself down from here. ¹⁰For it is written: "'He will command his angels concerning you to guard you carefully; ¹¹they will lift you up in their hands, so that you will not strike your foot against a stone.'"

¹²Jesus answered, "It says: 'Do not put the LORD your God to the test.'"

¹³When the devil had finished all this tempting, he left him until an opportune time.

Highlight the main and minor characters.

Where and when does this story take place?

What are the key events, activities, or ideas?

How did the characters respond? Why?

How is Jesus described (by Himself or others, claims made, character traits displayed)?

What values were taught/demonstrated by Jesus?

Beliefs (truths, principles taught or demonstrated by Jesus)

Conclusions (implications, if . . . then)

BACKGROUND

Jesus began His public ministry at about the age of thirty. Prior to that time He lived with His earthly parents, Joseph and Mary, in the town of Nazareth. Joseph was a carpenter so Jesus would have learned the trade as well.

The incident in the desert came early in Jesus' public ministry. He had been in the area of the Jordan River where John the Baptist ministered. There, John introduced Jesus to the crowds as "the lamb of God who takes away the sin of the world."

KEY WORDS

Devil: Chief of the fallen spirits. Chief adversary of God and man. Also called Satan.

Jordan: Only large flowing body of water in Israel. Connects Sea of Galilee with the Dead Sea.

Lord: Expresses a varied degree of honor, dignity, and majesty.

Scripture: Collection of holy, inspired writings.

Son of God: Term used to designate His coequal, eternal deity, and yet human nature.

Luke 4:14-30

¹⁴ Jesus returned to Galilee in the power of the Spirit, and news about him spread through the whole countryside. ¹⁵He taught in their synagogues, and everyone praised him.

¹⁶ He went to Nazareth, where he had been brought up, and on the Sabbath day he went into the synagogue, as was his custom. And he stood up to read. ¹⁷ The scroll of the prophet Isaiah was handed to him. Unrolling it, he found the place where it is written: ¹⁸ "The Spirit of the LORD is on me, because he has anointed me to preach good news to the poor. He has sent me to proclaim freedom for the prisoners and recovery of sight for the blind, to release the oppressed, ¹⁹ to proclaim the year of the LORD's favor."

²⁰ Then he rolled up the scroll, gave it back to the attendant and sat down. The eyes of everyone in the synagogue were fastened on him, ²¹ and he began by saying to them, "Today this scripture is fulfilled in your hearing."

²² All spoke well of him and were amazed at the gracious words that came from his lips. "Isn't this Joseph's son?" they asked.

²³ Jesus said to them, "Surely you will quote this proverb to me: 'Physician, heal yourself! Do here in your hometown what we have heard that you did in Capernaum.'"

²⁴ "I tell you the truth," he continued, "no prophet is accepted in his hometown. ²⁵ I assure you that there were many widows in Israel in Elijah's time, when the sky was shut for three and a half years and there was a severe famine throughout the land. ²⁶ Yet Elijah was not sent to any of them, but to a widow in Zarephath in the region of Sidon. ²⁷ And there were many in Israel with leprosy in the time of Elisha the prophet, yet not one of them was cleansed—only Naaman the Syrian."

²⁸ All the people in the synagogue were furious when they heard this. ²⁹ They got up, drove him out of the town, and took him to the brow of the hill on which the town was built, in order to throw him down the cliff. ³⁰ But he walked right through the crowd and went on his way.

Highlight the main and minor characters.

Where and when does this story take place?

What are the key events, activities, or ideas?

How did the characters respond? Why?

How is Jesus described (by Himself or others, claims made, character traits displayed)?

What values were taught/demonstrated by Jesus?

Beliefs (truths, principles taught or demonstrated by Jesus)

Conclusions (implications, if . . . then)

BACKGROUND

Jesus read from the Old Testament book of Isaiah. The passage dealt with the prophecy of a deliverer, a prophet . . . a Messiah. He claimed to be the fulfillment of that expectation.

KEY WORDS

Synagogue: Congregation of the Jews for the purpose of religious instruction and worship apart from the service of the temple.

Sabbath: The seventh day of the week (Saturday) celebrated as the day of rest and religious observation among the Jews.

Galilee: An ancient Roman province in Israel. An area north of Jerusalem that included the Sea of Galilee and Jesus' hometown.

Nazareth: A town in lower Galilee; hometown of Mary and Joseph and the town where Jesus grew up.

Isaiah: An Old Testament prophet. His Old Testament writings include many prophecies regarding the coming Messiah.

Capernaum: A town on the northwest shore of the Sea of Galilee where Jesus made His headquarters during His ministry in Galilee.

Elijah/Elisha: Old Testament prophets who conducted many miracles during their lifetimes.

Zarephath: An ancient Canaanite city near the coast north of Israel.

³¹ Then he went down to Capernaum, a town in Galilee, and on the Sabbath began to teach the people. ³² They were amazed at his teaching, because his message had authority.

³³ In the synagogue there was a man possessed by a demon, an evil spirit. He cried out at the top of his voice, ³⁴ "Ha! What do you want with us, Jesus of Nazareth? Have you come to destroy us? I know who you are—the Holy One of God!"

³⁵ "Be quiet!" Jesus said sternly. "Come out of him!" Then the demon threw the man down before them all and came out without injuring him.

³⁶ All the people were amazed and said to each other, "What is this teaching? With authority and power he gives orders to evil spirits and they come out!" ³⁷ And the news about him spread throughout the surrounding area.

³⁸ Jesus left the synagogue and went to the home of Simon. Now Simon's mother-in-law was suffering from a high fever, and they asked Jesus to help her. ³⁹ So he bent over her and rebuked the fever, and it left her. She got up at once and began to wait on them.

⁴⁰ When the sun was setting, the people brought to Jesus all who had various kinds of sickness, and laying his hands on each one, he healed them. ⁴¹ Moreover, demons came out of many people, shouting, "You are the Son of God!" But he rebuked them and would not allow them to speak, because they knew he was the Christ.

⁴² At daybreak Jesus went out to a solitary place. The people were looking for him and when they came to where he was, they tried to keep him from leaving them. ⁴³ But he said, "I must preach the good news of the kingdom of God to the other towns also, because that is why I was sent." ⁴⁴ And he kept on preaching in the synagogues of Judea.

Highlight the main and minor characters.

Where and when does this story take place?

What are the key events, activities, or ideas?

How did the characters respond? Why?

How is Jesus described (by Himself or others, claims made, character traits displayed)?

What values were taught/demonstrated by Jesus?

Beliefs (truths, principles taught or demonstrated by Jesus)

Conclusions (implications, if . . . then)

BACKGROUND

New Testament writers knew that people in their day attributed illness and abnormalities to both natural causes and demon possession. Demon possession was the control of a person by a foreign (evil) spirit.

The demonic spirit world realized Christ's divinity. But they were not certain of His purpose.

KEY WORDS

Simon: Also called Peter, one of the initial followers of Jesus and one of the twelve apostles.

Christ: Means "anointed one." Hebrew word was Messiah. Old Testament prophecy expected a deliverer who would bring about a new kingdom where peace and righteousness would reign.

Luke 5:1-11

[1] One day as Jesus was standing by the Lake of Gennesaret, with the people crowding around him and listening to the word of God, [2] he saw at the water's edge two boats, left there by the fishermen, who were washing their nets. [3] He got into one of the boats, the one belonging to Simon, and asked him to put out a little from shore. Then he sat down and taught the people from the boat.

[4] When he had finished speaking, he said to Simon, "Put out into deep water, and let down the nets for a catch."

[5] Simon answered, "Master, we've worked hard all night and haven't caught anything. But because you say so, I will let down the nets."

[6] When they had done so, they caught such a large number of fish that their nets began to break. [7] So they signaled their partners in the other boat to come and help them, and they came and filled both boats so full that they began to sink.

[8] When Simon Peter saw this, he fell at Jesus' knees and said, "Go away from me, LORD; I am a sinful man!" [9] For he and all his companions were astonished at the catch of fish they had taken, [10] and so were James and John, the sons of Zebedee, Simon's partners.

Then Jesus said to Simon, "Don't be afraid; from now on you will catch men." [11] So they pulled their boats up on shore, left everything and followed him.

Highlight the main and minor characters.

Where and when does this story take place?

What are the key events, activities, or ideas?

How did the characters respond? Why?

How is Jesus described (by Himself or others, claims made, character traits displayed)?

What values were taught/demonstrated by Jesus?

Beliefs (truths, principles taught or demonstrated by Jesus)

Conclusions (implications, if . . . then)

BACKGROUND

Jesus taught the crowds the word of God. His message was referred to as "the gospel of the kingdom," which dealt with the reign of God in the hearts and lives of people.

Jesus used any convenient spot to teach about the kingdom. Sometimes He taught in the synagogue. Yet more often He used people's natural surroundings. As well as being the center of activity, the lake served as a good acoustical background.

By the time Jesus asked Peter to go fishing it was probably noon. This was an unlikely time since the commercial fishermen had been out all night and were using the daytime for repairs.

Peter, James, and John had encountered Jesus before this. They traveled with Him in the preceding months as He taught in the vicinity of Jerusalem.

KEY WORDS

Lake Gennesaret: Same as the Sea of Galilee.

Simon: Also called Peter, one of the twelve apostles.

James and John: Brothers who also became part of the twelve apostles. Like Peter, they were fishermen by trade.

Master: Another title for rabbi. Rabbi was a title given by the Jews to the teachers of their law.

Luke 5:17-26

¹⁷ One day as he was teaching, Pharisees and teachers of the law, who had come from every village of Galilee and from Judea and Jerusalem, were sitting there. And the power of the LORD was present for him to heal the sick. ¹⁸ Some men came carrying a paralytic on a mat and tried to take him into the house to lay him before Jesus. ¹⁹ When they could not find a way to do this because of the crowd, they went up on the roof and lowered him on his mat through the tiles into the middle of the crowd, right in front of Jesus.

²⁰ When Jesus saw their faith, he said, "Friend, your sins are forgiven."

²¹ The Pharisees and the teachers of the law began thinking to themselves, "Who is this fellow who speaks blasphemy? Who can forgive sins but God alone?"

²² Jesus knew what they were thinking and asked, "Why are you thinking these things in your hearts? ²³ Which is easier: to say, 'Your sins are forgiven,' or to say, 'Get up and walk'?

²⁴ But that you may know that the Son of Man has authority on earth to forgive sins. . . ." He said to the paralyzed man, "I tell you, get up, take your mat and go home." ²⁵ Immediately he stood up in front of them, took what he had been lying on and went home praising God. ²⁶ Everyone was amazed and gave praise to God. They were filled with awe and said, "We have seen remarkable things today."

Highlight the main and minor characters.

Where and when does this story take place?

What are the key events, activities, or ideas?

How did the characters respond? Why?

How is Jesus described (by Himself or others, claims made, character traits displayed)?

What values were taught/demonstrated by Jesus?

Beliefs (truths, principles taught or demonstrated by Jesus)

Conclusions (implications, if . . . then)

BACKGROUND

This incident takes place at a house in Capernaum. Capernaum was the head-quarters of Jesus' ministry in Galilee. The house was filled with a variety of people who listened and watched. The Pharisees observed Jesus to determine if His claims were legitimate.

KEY WORDS

Pharisees: The most strict and influential of three prominent societies of Judaism at the time of Christ. They were experts in the interpretation of Scripture and were considered the religious leaders.

Teachers of the Law: Often called scribes, these men studied, taught, interpreted, and transmitted the Mosaic Law. God's real law was often buried beneath tradition.

Blasphemy: To speak lightly or carelessly of God was a mortal sin. In Israel the penalty was death by stoning.

Son of Man: A phrase used by Christ to describe Himself. It had its roots in the Old Testament and referred to the One who was coming again to rule the world.

Luke 5:27-38

27 After this, Jesus went out and saw a tax collector by the name of Levi sitting at his tax booth. "Follow me," Jesus said to him, 28 and Levi got up, left everything and followed him.

29 Then Levi held a great banquet for Jesus at his house, and a large crowd of tax collectors and others were eating with them. 30 But the Pharisees and the teachers of the law who belonged to their sect complained to his disciples, "Why do you eat and drink with tax collectors and 'sinners'?"

31 Jesus answered them, "It is not the healthy who need a doctor, but the sick. 32 I have not come to call the righteous, but sinners to repentance."

33 They said to him, "John's disciples often fast and pray, and so do the disciples of the Pharisees, but yours go on eating and drinking."

34 Jesus answered, "Can you make the guests of the bridegroom fast while he is with them? 35 But the time will come when the bridegroom will be taken from them; in those days they will fast."

36 He told them this parable: "No one tears a patch from a new garment and sews it on an old one. If he does, he will have torn the new garment, and the patch from the new will not match the old. 37 And no one pours new wine into old wineskins. If he does, the new wine will burst the skins, the wine will run out and the wineskins will be ruined. 38 No, new wine must be poured into new wineskins."

Highlight the main and minor characters.

Where and when does this story take place?

What are the key events, activities, or ideas?

How did the characters respond? Why?

How is Jesus described (by Himself or others, claims made, character traits displayed)?

What values were taught/demonstrated by Jesus?

Beliefs (truths, principles taught or demonstrated by Jesus)

Conclusions (implications, if . . . then)

BACKGROUND

Tax collectors were outcasts. People considered them traitors and extortionists. The religious elite such as the Pharisees and scribes found them particularly distasteful.

The Pharisees and scribes had, in their zeal to be holy to God, created an elaborate system of rules and traditions that went beyond Old Testament Scripture. They now considered these traditions as authoritative as Scripture. Jesus rejected and attacked this system, and consequently He incurred the constant scrutiny and wrath of the religious elite.

KEY WORDS

Tax collector: One who collected tolls for the Roman government on merchandise passing through the area. Tax collectors were known for graft and corruption. Jews who were so employed were also regarded as traitors.

Levi: A Jew; also called Matthew; became one of the twelve apostles.

Sinners: People who "miss the mark" in terms of God's standards.

Righteous: In this instance, those who mistakenly considered themselves worthy.

Repentance: Conversion; a complete transformation; change of mind, heart, will, and conduct.

John's disciples: John the Baptist was Jesus' cousin. John had a ministry of prophecy, announcing that the "kingdom of God is at hand."

Fast: A voluntary abstaining from food for a period of time for religious purposes.

²⁰ Looking at his disciples, he said: "Blessed are you who are poor [in spirit], for yours is the kingdom of God. . . ."
²⁷ "But I tell you who hear me: Love your enemies, do good to those who hate you, ³¹ Do to others as you would have them do to you. . . . ³⁶ Be merciful, just as your Father is merciful. ³⁸ Give, and it will be given to you. A good measure, pressed down, shaken together and running over, will be poured into your lap. For with the measure you use, it will be measured to you. . . ."

³⁹ He also told them this parable: "Can a blind man lead a blind man? Will they not both fall into a pit? ⁴⁰ A student is not above his teacher, but everyone who is fully trained will be like his teacher.

⁴¹ "Why do you look at the speck of sawdust in your brother's eye and pay no attention to the plank in your own eye? ⁴² How can you say to your brother, 'Brother, let me take the speck out of your eye,' when you yourself fail to see the plank in your own eye? You hypocrite, first take the plank out of your eye, and then you will see clearly to remove the speck from your brother's eye.

⁴³ "No good tree bears bad fruit, nor does a bad tree bear good fruit. ⁴⁴ Each tree is recognized by its own fruit. People do not pick figs from thornbushes, or grapes from briers. ⁴⁵ The good man brings good things out of the good stored up in his heart, and the evil man brings evil things out of evil stored up in his heart. For out of the overflow of his heart his mouth speaks.

⁴⁶ "Why do you call me, 'LORD, LORD,' and do not do what I say? ⁴⁷ I will show you what he is like who comes to me and hears my words and puts them into practice. ⁴⁸ He is like a man building a house, who dug down deep and laid the foundation on rock. When a flood came, the torrent struck that house but could not shake it, because it was well built. ⁴⁹ But the one who hears my words and does not put them into practice is like a man who built a house on the ground without a foundation. The moment the torrent struck that house, it collapsed and its destruction was complete."

Highlight the main and minor characters.

Where and when does this story take place?

What are the key events, activities, or ideas?

How did the characters respond? Why?

How is Jesus described (by Himself or others, claims made, character traits displayed)?

What values were taught/demonstrated by Jesus?

Beliefs (truths, principles taught or demonstrated by Jesus)

Conclusions (implications, if . . . then)

BACKGROUND

In this message, Jesus summarized for His followers how to live as part of His kingdom. He delivered it on a mountain hillside, and it is commonly referred to as the "Sermon on the Mount."

Although given primarily to His followers, the intended application was for all who would listen.

KEY WORDS

Disciple: A follower of Jesus. Some were more committed than others. Earlier in this same day, Jesus had selected twelve men who were the core group of His disciples.

Poor: Spiritual poverty, not material poverty; poor toward God; those who recognize their spiritual bankruptcy.

Heart: The core of a person's being.

Beam: Heavy piece of wood used for rafters in building.

Speck: Small piece of wood or straw.

Luke 7:1-10

[1] When Jesus had finished saying all this in the hearing of the people, he entered Capernaum. [2] There a centurion's servant, whom his master valued highly, was sick and about to die. [3] The centurion heard of Jesus and sent some elders of the Jews to him, asking him to come and heal his servant. [4] When they came to Jesus, they pleaded earnestly with him, "This man deserves to have you do this, [5] because he loves our nation and has built our synagogue." [6] So Jesus went with them.

He was not far from the house when the centurion sent friends to say to him: "LORD, don't trouble yourself, for I do not deserve to have you come under my roof. [7] That is why I did not even consider myself worthy to come to you. But say the word, and my servant will be healed. [8] For I myself am a man under authority, with soldiers under me. I tell this one, 'Go,' and he goes; and that one, 'Come,' and he comes. I say to my servant, 'Do this,' and he does it."

[9] When Jesus heard this, he was amazed at him, and turning to the crowd following him, he said, "I tell you, I have not found such great faith even in Israel." [10] Then the men who had been sent returned to the house and found the servant well.

Highlight the main and minor characters.

Where and when does this story take place?

What are the key events, activities, or ideas?

How did the characters respond? Why?

How is Jesus described (by Himself or others, claims made, character traits displayed)?

What values were taught/demonstrated by Jesus?

Beliefs (truths, principles taught or demonstrated by Jesus)

Conclusions (implications, if . . . then)

KEY WORDS

Capernaum: A city in the province of Galilee. Jesus used it as His base of operations as He ministered in the province.

Centurion: A commander of one hundred soldiers in the Roman army.

Synagogue: A congregation of the Jews for the purpose of religious instruction and worship apart from the service of the temple.

36 Now one of the Pharisees invited Jesus to have dinner with him, so he went to the Pharisee's house and reclined at the table. 37 When a woman who had lived a sinful life in that town learned that Jesus was eating at the Pharisee's house, she brought an alabaster jar of perfume, 38 and as she stood behind him at his feet weeping, she began to wet his feet with her tears. Then she wiped them with her hair, kissed them and poured perfume on them.

39 When the Pharisee who had invited him saw this, he said to himself, "If this man were a prophet, he would know who is touching him and what kind of woman she is—that she is a sinner."

40 Jesus answered him, "Simon, I have something to tell you."

"Tell me, teacher," he said.

41 "Two men owed money to a certain moneylender. One owed him five hundred denarii, and the other fifty. 42 Neither of them had the money to pay him back, so he canceled the debts of both. Now which of them will love him more?"

43 Simon replied, "I suppose the one who had the bigger debt canceled."

"You have judged correctly," Jesus said.

44 Then he turned toward the woman and said to Simon, "Do you see this woman? I came into your house. You did not give me any water for my feet, but she wet my feet with her tears and wiped them with her hair. 45 You did not give me a kiss, but this woman, from the time I entered, has not stopped kissing my feet. 46 You did not put oil on my head, but she has poured perfume on my feet. 47 Therefore, I tell you, her many sins have been forgiven—for she loved much. But he who has been forgiven little loves little."

48 Then Jesus said to her, "Your sins are forgiven."

49 The other guests began to say among themselves, "Who is this who even forgives sins?"

50 Jesus said to the woman, "Your faith has saved you; go in peace."

Highlight the main and minor characters.

Where and when does this story take place?

What are the key events, activities, or ideas?

How did the characters respond? Why?

How is Jesus described (by Himself or others, claims made, character traits displayed)?

What values were taught/demonstrated by Jesus?

Beliefs (truths, principles taught or demonstrated by Jesus)

Conclusions (implications, if . . . then)

BACKGROUND

People usually ate their meal in a reclining position on low couches around the table. Their head would face the table, their feet extending backward.

Uninvited guests often came to a dinner party and sat around the wall of the room and observed—and sometimes even entered into the conversation.

Hosts greeted invited guests with a kiss, foot washing, and oil for anointing their head. Simon's treatment of Jesus would have been considered cold and discourteous.

It was not considered proper at this time for a woman to let her hair down in public.

KEY WORDS

Pharisee: This Simon was not the same as Peter the apostle.

Alabaster jar: Vase of expensive, white perfume; a fine-grained gypsum. It was often used as an offering of thanksgiving.

Denari: A day's wage for a common laborer in Jesus' time.

Woman/a sinner: One with a bad reputation, could have been for a variety of reasons.

⁴⁰ Now when Jesus returned, a crowd welcomed him, for they were all expecting him. ⁴¹ Then a man named Jairus, a ruler of the synagogue, came and fell at Jesus' feet, pleading with him to come to his house ⁴² because his only daughter, a girl of about twelve, was dying.

As Jesus was on his way, the crowds almost crushed him. ⁴³ And a woman was there who had been subject to bleeding for twelve years, but no one could heal her. ⁴⁴ She came up behind him and touched the edge of his cloak, and immediately her bleeding stopped.

⁴⁵ "Who touched me?" Jesus asked.

When they all denied it, Peter said, "Master, the people are crowding and pressing against you."

⁴⁶ But Jesus said, "Someone touched me; I know that power has gone out from me."

⁴⁷ Then the woman, seeing that she could not go unnoticed, came trembling and fell at his feet. In the presence of all the people, she told why she had touched him and how she had been instantly healed. ⁴⁸ Then he said to her, "Daughter, your faith has healed you. Go in peace."

⁴⁹ While Jesus was still speaking, someone came from the house of Jairus, the synagogue ruler. "Your daughter is dead," he said. "Don't bother the teacher any more."

⁵⁰ Hearing this, Jesus said to Jairus, "Don't be afraid; just believe, and she will be healed." ⁵¹ When he arrived at the house of Jairus, he did not let anyone go in with him except Peter, John and James, and the child's father and mother. ⁵² Meanwhile, all the people were wailing and mourning for her. "Stop wailing," Jesus said. "She is not dead but asleep." ⁵³ They laughed at him, knowing that she was dead. ⁵⁴ But he took her by the hand and said, "My child, get up!" ⁵⁵ Her spirit returned, and at once she stood up. Then Jesus told them to give her something to eat. ⁵⁶ Her parents were astonished, but he ordered them not to tell anyone what had happened.

Highlight the main and minor characters.

Where and when does this story take place?

What are the key events, activities, or ideas?

How did the characters respond? Why?

How is Jesus described (by Himself or others, claims made, character traits displayed)?

What values were taught/demonstrated by Jesus?

Beliefs (truths, principles taught or demonstrated by Jesus)

BACKGROUND

Jesus had just returned from the eastern side of the Sea of Galilee where He healed a demon-possessed man. In response, the people there asked Jesus to leave. As a result, He returned to the area of Capernaum on the western shore.

The synagogue was the local place for worship and religious instruction. Jarius held a position of high social and religious standing as a member of its ruling board of elders.

The woman with the bleeding is not named. The therapeutics of the day could not heal her problem, and after twelve years of seeking treatment, she had used up her monetary resources. The religious code of the day considered her illness "ceremonially unclean." This implies she had also lost her social standing in the community.

Women did not speak in public in that culture. For this woman to do so required great risk and courage.

The wailing people at Jarius' home were part of the traditional funeral observance. Families often hired professional mourners. This group seemed especially large and unruly, possibly due to Jarius' status in the community.

Luke 9:18-27

¹⁸ Once when Jesus was praying in private and his disciples were with him, he asked them, "Who do the crowds say I am?"

¹⁹ They replied, "Some say John the Baptist; others say Elijah; and still others, that one of the prophets of long ago has come back to life."

²⁰ "But what about you?" he asked. "Who do you say I am?"

Peter answered, "The Christ of God."

²¹ Jesus strictly warned them not to tell this to anyone. ²² And he said, "The Son of Man must suffer many things and be rejected by the elders, chief priests and teachers of the law, and he must be killed and on the third day be raised to life."

²³ Then he said to them all: "If anyone would come after me, he must deny himself and take up his cross daily and follow me. ²⁴ For whoever wants to save his life will lose it, but whoever loses his life for me will save it. ²⁵ What good is it for a man to gain the whole world, and yet lose or forfeit his very self? ²⁶ If anyone is ashamed of me and my words, the Son of Man will be ashamed of him when he comes in his glory and in the glory of the Father and of the holy angels. ²⁷ I tell you the truth, some who are standing here will not taste death before they see the kingdom of God."

Highlight the main and minor characters.

Where and when does this story take place?

What are the key events, activities, or ideas?

How did the characters respond? Why?

How is Jesus described (by Himself or others, claims made, character traits displayed)?

What values were taught/demonstrated by Jesus?

Beliefs (truths, principles taught or demonstrated by Jesus)

Conclusions (implications, if . . . then)

BACKGROUND

Jesus traveled with His twelve disciples in the area of Caesarea Philippi, twenty-four miles north of Capernaum.

Jesus restrained the public proclamation of His claim as Messiah possibly due to the people's enthusiasm for a political deliverer from the oppression and domination of Rome.

KEY WORDS

John the Baptist: John was Jesus' cousin and had a primary mission of declaring that the kingdom of God was at hand. He introduced Jesus earlier as "the Lamb of God who takes away the sin of the world." John had recently been executed by Herod.

Elijah: A famous Old Testament prophet who had done many miracles during his life.

Christ: A title meaning Messiah, God's anointed, the long-awaited One. The Old Testament Jewish expectation for a coming Messiah incorporated a Mediator as Chief Prophet, only High Priest, and Eternal King.

Son of Man: An Old Testament title Jesus frequently used for Himself, which conveyed both His deity and humanity. It was not as inflammatory as Messiah.

Elders, chief priests, and teachers of the Law: Privileged religious rulers and theologians responsible for the religious interests and welfare of the people.

Kingdom of God: Used in various ways but always implying "that where God rules." Here Jesus is referring to that new historical reality that would result from and directly follow His death and resurrection.

Luke 9:28-36

[28] About eight days after Jesus said this, he took Peter, John and James with him and went up onto a mountain to pray. [29] As he was praying, the appearance of his face changed, and his clothes became as bright as a flash of lightning. [30] Two men, Moses and Elijah, [31] appeared in glorious splendor, talking with Jesus. They spoke about his departure, which he was about to bring to fulfillment at Jerusalem. [32] Peter and his companions were very sleepy, but when they became fully awake, they saw his glory and the two men standing with him. [33] As the men were leaving Jesus, Peter said to him, "Master, it is good for us to be here. Let us put up three shelters—one for you, one for Moses and one for Elijah." (He did not know what he was saying.)

[34] While he was speaking, a cloud appeared and enveloped them, and they were afraid as they entered the cloud. [35] A voice came from the cloud, saying, "This is my Son, whom I have chosen; listen to him." [36] When the voice had spoken, they found that Jesus was alone. The disciples kept this to themselves, and told no one at that time what they had seen.

Highlight the main and minor characters.

Where and when does this story take place?

What are the key events, activities, or ideas?

How did the characters respond? Why?

How is Jesus described (by Himself or others, claims made, character traits displayed)?

What values were taught/demonstrated by Jesus?

Beliefs (truths, principles taught or demonstrated by Jesus)

Conclusions (implications, if . . . then)

BACKGROUND

The departure Jesus discussed refers to His death, burial, and resurrection that were about to happen in Jerusalem.

The shelters likely represented Peter's attempt to prolong Jesus' stay. Yet Jesus kept steadily moving toward His goals.

Moses and Elijah traditionally represented the Law and the Prophets respectively, the two pillars upon which the Jewish faith rested.

KEY WORDS

Peter, James, and John: These men were the most visible of the twelve disciples. They often accompanied Jesus on key events.

Moses: Old Testament character who led Israel from slavery in Egypt to freedom. He was responsible for giving Israel the Law of God.

Elijah: Key Old Testament prophet.

Master: Lord, rabbi, teacher, title of deep respect.

Luke 10:25-37

25 On one occasion an expert in the law stood up to test Jesus. "Teacher," he asked, "what must I do to inherit eternal life?"

26 "What is written in the Law?" he replied. "How do you read it?"

27 He answered: "'Love the LORD your God with all your heart and with all your soul and with all your strength and with all your mind'; and, 'Love your neighbor as yourself.'"

28 "You have answered correctly," Jesus replied. "Do this and you will live."

29 But he wanted to justify himself, so he asked Jesus, "And who is my neighbor?"

30 In reply Jesus said: "A man was going down from Jerusalem to Jericho, when he fell into the hands of robbers. They stripped him of his clothes, beat him and went away, leaving him half dead. 31 A priest happened to be going down the same road, and when he saw the man, he passed by on the other side. 32 So too, a Levite, when he came to the place and saw him, passed by on the other side. 33 But a Samaritan, as he traveled, came where the man was; and when he saw him, he took pity on him. 34 He went to him and bandaged his wounds, pouring on oil and wine. Then he put the man on his own donkey, took him to an inn and took care of him. 35 The next day he took out two silver coins and gave them to the innkeeper. 'Look after him,' he said, 'and when I return, I will reimburse you for any extra expense you may have.'

36 "Which of these three do you think was a neighbor to the man who fell into the hands of robbers?"

37 The expert in the law replied, "The one who had mercy on him." Jesus told him, "Go and do likewise."

Highlight the main and minor characters.

Where and when does this story take place?

What are the key events, activities, or ideas?

How did the characters respond? Why?

How is Jesus described (by Himself or others, claims made, character traits displayed)?

What values were taught/demonstrated by Jesus?

Beliefs (truths, principles taught or demonstrated by Jesus)

Conclusions (implications, if . . . then)

BACKGROUND

This religious lawyer stated the requirements of the law. The demand was for perfect compliance to God's standard of absolute love of both God and others. The lawyer recognized these implications and sought to justify himself by limiting his responsibility.

The law was not given as a means of obtaining right standing with God. It was given to show God's high moral nature and to teach man's inability to attain God's standard of righteousness. Romans 3:20 states, "Therefore, no one will be declared righteous in his [God's] sight by observing the law; rather, through the law we become conscious of sin."

KEY WORDS

Eternal life: Refers to both duration and quality.

Jerusalem to Jericho: A seventeen-mile trip through rugged, rocky, dangerous terrain. Robbers would often victimize even wary travelers.

Priest/Levite: Those who served in the temple. They were of the official religious order, probably on their way home after fulfilling their temple duty in Jerusalem.

Samaritan: A group of people who were ethnically half Jew and half Gentile. There was a mutually hostile/hate relationship between the Jews and Samaritans. A Jew at that time would have considered a "good Samaritan" an impossibility.

15 Then he said to them, "Watch out! Be on your guard against all kinds of greed; a man's life does not consist in the abundance of his possessions."

16 And he told them this parable: "The ground of a certain rich man produced a good crop. 17 He thought to himself, 'What shall I do? I have no place to store my crops.'

18 "Then he said, 'This is what I'll do. I will tear down my barns and build bigger ones, and there I will store all my grain and my goods. 19 And I'll say to myself, "You have plenty of good things laid up for many years. Take life easy; eat, drink and be merry."'

20 "But God said to him, 'You fool! This very night your life will be demanded from you. Then who will get what you have prepared for yourself?'

21 "This is how it will be with anyone who stores up things for himself but is not rich toward God."

22 Then Jesus said to his disciples: "Therefore I tell you, do not worry about your life, what you will eat; or about your body, what you will wear. 23 Life is more than food, and the body more than clothes. 24 Consider the ravens: They do not sow or reap, they have no storeroom or barn; yet God feeds them. And how much more valuable you are than birds! 25 Who of you by worrying can add a single hour to his life? 26 Since you cannot do this very little thing, why do you worry about the rest?

27 "Consider how the lilies grow. They do not labor or spin. Yet I tell you, not even Solomon in all his splendor was dressed like one of these. 28 If that is how God clothes the grass of the field, which is here today, and tomorrow is thrown into the fire, how much more will he clothe you, O you of little faith! 29 And do not set your heart on what you will eat or drink; do not worry about it. 30 For the pagan world runs after all such things, and your Father knows that you need them. 31 But seek his kingdom, and these things will be given to you as well.

32 "Do not be afraid, little flock, for your Father has been pleased to give you the kingdom. 33 Sell your possessions and give to the poor. Provide purses for yourselves that will not wear out, a treasure in heaven that will not be exhausted, where no thief comes near and no moth destroys. 34 For where your treasure is, there your heart will be also."

Highlight the main and minor characters.

Where and when does this story take place?

What are the key events, activities, or ideas?

How did the characters respond? Why?

How is Jesus described (by Himself or others, claims made, character traits displayed)?

What values were taught/demonstrated by Jesus?

Beliefs (truths, principles taught or demonstrated by Jesus)

Conclusions (implications, if . . . then)

BACKGROUND

Jesus taught the crowds in general but addressed the twelve disciples in particular.

When Jesus made the statement to "sell your possessions and give to the poor," it was in the context of the rich/foolish man who hoarded all his wealth. Jesus did not say to "sell **all** your possessions and give the **entire** amount to the poor" as some have misinterpreted His teaching throughout history.

A person's treasure is that for which he or she ultimately strives. It could include power, prestige, and wealth.

KEY WORDS

Greed: The thirst for having more.

Solomon: An important king of Israel and son to King David. Solomon was the king who built Israel into a wealthy, respected, and prosperous nation. He built the original temple that was later destroyed and subsequently rebuilt.

Pagan world: Term for the unbeliever in contrast to the believers or disciples.

Luke 14:15-24

15 When one of those at the table with him heard this, he said to Jesus, "Blessed is the man who will eat at the feast in the kingdom of God."

16 Jesus replied: "A certain man was preparing a great banquet and invited many guests. 17 At the time of the banquet he sent his servant to tell those who had been invited, 'Come, for everything is now ready.'

18 "But they all alike began to make excuses. The first said, 'I have just bought a field, and I must go and see it. Please excuse me.'

19 Another said, 'I have just bought five yoke of oxen, and I'm on my way to try them out. Please excuse me.'

20 "Still another said, 'I just got married, so I can't come.'

21 "The servant came back and reported this to his master. Then the owner of the house became angry and ordered his servant, 'Go out quickly into the streets and alleys of the town and bring in the poor, the crippled, the blind and the lame.'

22 " 'Sir,' the servant said, 'what you ordered has been done, but there is still room.'

23 "Then the master told his servant, 'Go out to the roads and country lanes and make them come in, so that my house will be full. 24 I tell you, not one of those men who were invited will get a taste of my banquet.'"

Highlight the main and minor characters.

Where and when does this story take place?

What are the key events, activities, or ideas?

How did the characters respond? Why?

How is Jesus described (by Himself or others, claims made, character traits displayed)?

What values were taught/demonstrated by Jesus?

Beliefs (truths, principles taught or demonstrated by Jesus)

Conclusions (implications, if . . . then)

BACKGROUND

Eating at the home of a prominent Pharisee, Jesus discussed the merits and demonstration of humility. Those in attendance obviously sought positions of power and prestige. Jesus challenged his host to give a banquet and invite those who could not repay the favor. He said the reward for such action would not come from the guests themselves but at the resurrection of the righteous.

It was in reference to this "resurrection of the righteous" that a guest made the initial statement in this story.

Jesus referred to the future joys and delights of eternal life as the feast in the kingdom of God. He did not give details of what this future life would entail. He did, however, picture it as a banquet. In the broadest terms, the banquet represented the joyful communion of God and His people for eternity.

It is in reference to this great banquet that Jesus tells an additional parable.

The double invitation was common in Jesus' day. The guests had been invited and were being reminded. Even though they were being reminded, the initial guests refused to come. Most likely Jesus is referring to the Jews of that generation who refused to respond in belief to His invitation and claims.

As a result, He would extend the invitation to the Gentiles as well. Those now invited represented the undeserving and unlikely.

[11] Jesus continued: "There was a man who had two sons. [12] The younger one said to his father, 'Father, give me my share of the estate.' So he divided his property between them.

[13] "Not long after that, the younger son got together all he had, set off for a distant country and there squandered his wealth in wild living. [14] After he had spent everything, there was a severe famine in that whole country, and he began to be in need. [15] So he went and hired himself out to a citizen of that country, who sent him to his fields to feed pigs. [16] He longed to fill his stomach with the pods that the pigs were eating, but no one gave him anything.

[17] "When he came to his senses, he said, 'How many of my father's hired men have food to spare, and here I am starving to death! [18] I will set out and go back to my father and say to him: Father, I have sinned against heaven and against you. [19] I am no longer worthy to be called your son; make me like one of your hired men.' [20] So he got up and went to his father.

"But while he was still a long way off, his father saw him and was filled with compassion for him; he ran to his son, threw his arms around him and kissed him.

[21] "The son said to him, 'Father, I have sinned against heaven and against you. I am no longer worthy to be called your son.'

[22] "But the father said to his servants, 'Quick! Bring the best robe and put it on him. Put a ring on his finger and sandals on his feet. [23] Bring the fattened calf and kill it. Let's have a feast and celebrate. [24] For this son of mine was dead and is alive again; he was lost and is found.' So they began to celebrate.

[25] "Meanwhile, the older son was in the field. When he came near the house, he heard music and dancing. [26] So he called one of the servants and asked him what was going on. [27] 'Your brother has come,' he replied, 'and your father has killed the fattened calf because he has him back safe and sound.'

[28] "The older brother became angry and refused to go in. So his father went out and pleaded with him. [29] But he answered his father, 'Look! All these years I've been slaving for you and never disobeyed your orders. Yet you never gave me even a young goat so I could celebrate with my friends. [30] But when this son of yours who has squandered your property with prostitutes comes home, you kill the fattened calf for him!'

[31] "'My son,' the father said, 'you are always with me, and everything I have is yours. [32] But we had to celebrate and be glad, because this brother of yours was dead and is alive again; he was lost and is found.'"

Highlight the main and minor characters.

Where and when does this story take place?

What are the key events, activities, or ideas?

How did the characters respond? Why?

How is Jesus described (by Himself or others, claims made, character traits displayed)?

What values were taught/demonstrated by Jesus?

Beliefs (truths, principles taught or demonstrated by Jesus)

Conclusions (implications, if . . . then)

BACKGROUND

According to Old Testament law, the younger son inherited one-third of the parental estate upon his father's death. Two-thirds would go to the elder son. In this case, the father probably divided up the property and sold a portion for cash to accommodate the younger son's request.

According to Jewish custom, it was a curse to take care of pigs. The job of feeding pigs would have been considered the lowest point of humiliation.

A hired man was usually a day laborer. The term didn't even apply to a full-time servant.

The best robe, ring, and sandals were symbols of authority. He was not to be a servant but a freeman.

Hosts reserved the fatted calf for special occasions when important guests were expected.

Luke 17:20-35

20 Once, having been asked by the Pharisees when the kingdom of God would come, Jesus replied, "The kingdom of God does not come with your careful observation, 21 nor will people say, 'Here it is,' or 'There it is,' because the kingdom of God is among you."

22 Then he said to his disciples, "The time is coming when you will long to see one of the days of the Son of Man, but you will not see it. 23 Men will tell you, 'There he is!' or 'Here he is!' Do not go running off after them. 24 For the Son of Man in his day will be like the lightning, which flashes and lights up the sky from one end to the other. 25 But first he must suffer many things and be rejected by this generation.

26 "Just as it was in the days of Noah, so also will it be in the days of the Son of Man. 27 People were eating, drinking, marrying and being given in marriage up to the day Noah entered the ark. Then the flood came and destroyed them all.

28 "It was the same in the days of Lot. People were eating and drinking, buying and selling, planting and building. 29 But the day Lot left Sodom, fire and sulfur rained down from heaven and destroyed them all.

30 "It will be just like this on the day the Son of Man is revealed. 31 On that day no one who is on the roof of his house, with his goods inside, should go down to get them. Likewise, no one in the field should go back for anything. 32 Remember Lot's wife! 33 Whoever tries to keep his life will lose it, and whoever loses his life will preserve it. 34 I tell you, on that night two people will be in one bed; one will be taken and the other left. 35 Two women will be grinding grain together; one will be taken and the other left."

Highlight the main and minor characters.

Where and when does this story take place?

What are the key events, activities, or ideas?

How did the characters respond? Why?

How is Jesus described (by Himself or others, claims made, character traits displayed)?

What values were taught/demonstrated by Jesus?

Beliefs (truths, principles taught or demonstrated by Jesus)

Conclusions (implications, if . . . then)

BACKGROUND

The kingdom of God was a concept that was prominent in Jewish thought. At this point in history, the Jews anticipated a physical, visible, earthly kingdom in which they would have a key role. *Kingdom* can be used to mean either kingdom or kingship/reign.

KEY WORDS

Pharisees: The most strict and influential of Jewish religious leaders.

Son of Man: An Old Testament title for the One who was to come and rule. Jesus frequently used this title for Himself.

Noah: The one righteous person who, along with his family, survived the great flood in the Old Testament.

Lot: The nephew of Abraham. Lot lived in the wicked city of Sodom. God destroyed the city but Lot was spared. Lot's wife also escaped the city but in disobeying God's command not to look back, she turned into a pillar of salt.

Luke 23:1-7, 13-25

[1] Then the whole assembly rose and led him off to Pilate. [2] And they began to accuse him, saying, "We have found this man subverting our nation. He opposes payment of taxes to Caesar and claims to be Christ, a king."

[3] So Pilate asked Jesus, "Are you the king of the Jews?"

"Yes, it is as you say," Jesus replied.

[4] Then Pilate announced to the chief priests and the crowd, "I find no basis for a charge against this man."

[5] But they insisted, "He stirs up the people all over Judea by his teaching. He started in Galilee and has come all the way here."

[6] On hearing this, Pilate asked if the man was a Galilean. [7] When he learned that Jesus was under Herod's jurisdiction, he sent him to Herod, who was also in Jerusalem at that time. . . .

[13] Pilate called together the chief priests, the rulers and the people, [14] and said to them, "You brought me this man as one who was inciting the people to rebellion. I have examined him in your presence and have found no basis for your charges against him. [15] Neither has Herod, for he sent him back to us; as you can see, he has done nothing to deserve death. [16] Therefore, I will punish him and then release him. . . ."

[18] With one voice they cried out, "Away with this man! Release Barabbas to us!" [19] (Barabbas had been thrown into prison for an insurrection in the city, and for murder.)

[20] Wanting to release Jesus, Pilate appealed to them again. [21] But they kept shouting, "Crucify him! Crucify him!"

[22] For the third time he spoke to them: "Why? What crime has this man committed? I have found in him no grounds for the death penalty. Therefore I will have him punished and then release him."

[23] But with loud shouts they insistently demanded that he be crucified, and their shouts prevailed. [24] So Pilate decided to grant their demand. [25] He released the man who had been thrown into prison for insurrection and murder, the one they asked for, and surrendered Jesus to their will.

Highlight the main and minor characters.

Where and when does this story take place?

What are the key events, activities, or ideas?

How did the characters respond? Why?

How is Jesus described (by Himself or others, claims made, character traits displayed)?

What values were taught/demonstrated by Jesus?

Beliefs (truths, principles taught or demonstrated by Jesus)

Conclusions (implications, if . . . then)

BACKGROUND

Jesus had been arrested during the night and brought before the Jewish high priest for a religious trial. That court accused Him of breaking traditional religious laws. Failing to present a legitimate case, they raised the issue of blasphemy, His claim to be equal with God. Under oath, they asked Jesus, "Are you the Son of God?" He replied affirmatively. They responded by demanding his death.

The Jewish law carried out the death penalty by stoning. But in A.D. 30, Rome had removed the death penalty from Jewish control. The Romans crucified non-Romans.

Failing to have the power of death, the Jewish leaders turned to Rome to have their desire carried out. Therefore, they took Jesus to Pilate and created a civil case against Him, using lies designed to appeal to the governor's interests.

Political conditions in Rome left Pilate insecure and his loyalty to Rome suspect. As the crowds threatened him with rioting and charges of treason to Rome, Pilate gave in to their demands.

Under the tradition of releasing one prisoner as a mark of goodwill, Pilate tried to appease the Jewish leadership. They rejected his gesture.

KEY WORDS

Pilate: The Roman procurator of the provinces of Judea and Samaria.

Herod (Antipas): The ruler of the province of Galilee. He happened to be in Jerusalem at the time of this trial.

Chief priests and rulers: The Jewish leadership that conducted the late-night trial of Jesus and demanded His death.

[32] Two other men, both criminals, were also led out with him to be executed. [33] When they came to the place called the Skull, there they crucified him, along with the criminals—one on his right, the other on his left. [34] Jesus said, "Father, forgive them, for they do not know what they are doing." And they divided up his clothes by casting lots.

[35] The people stood watching, and the rulers even sneered at him. They said, "He saved others; let him save himself if he is the Christ of God, the Chosen One."

[36] The soldiers also came up and mocked him. They offered him wine vinegar [37] and said, "If you are the king of the Jews, save yourself."

[38] There was a written notice above him, which read: THIS IS THE KING OF THE JEWS.

[39] One of the criminals who hung there hurled insults at him: "Aren't you the Christ? Save yourself and us!"

[40] But the other criminal rebuked him. "Don't you fear God," he said, "since you are under the same sentence? [41] We are punished justly, for we are getting what our deeds deserve. But this man has done nothing wrong."

[42] Then he said, "Jesus, remember me when you come into your kingdom."

[43] Jesus answered him, "I tell you the truth, today you will be with me in paradise."

[44] It was now about the sixth hour, and darkness came over the whole land until the ninth hour, [45] for the sun stopped shining. And the curtain of the temple was torn in two. [46] Jesus called out with a loud voice, "Father, into your hands I commit my spirit." When he had said this, he breathed his last.

[47] The centurion, seeing what had happened, praised God and said, "Surely this was a righteous man."

Highlight the main and minor characters.

Where and when does this story take place?

What are the key events, activities, or ideas?

How did the characters respond? Why?

How is Jesus described (by Himself or others, claims made, character traits displayed)?

What values were taught/demonstrated by Jesus?

Beliefs (truths, principles taught or demonstrated by Jesus)

Conclusions (implications, if . . . then)

BACKGROUND

The superscription over Jesus' head read in Aramaic, Latin, and Greek: "This is Jesus of Nazareth the King of the Jews." Normally the superscription noted the crime. Pilate gave this title as a response to the Jewish leaders' accusations.

Various groups of people mocked Jesus in two common ways:

a. They mocked His claim of Messiah.

b. They challenged Him to come down from the cross.

The gospel accounts record three events at the time of Jesus' death. The Jewish temple veil was torn from top to bottom, signifying access to God by all people through Christ. There was a significant earthquake, and tombs of recently deceased saints were opened.

KEY WORDS

Place called the Skull: It was the location of Christ's execution. The exact location is not known. It was near Jerusalem and outside the city.

Casting lots: Probably throwing dice, lottery system. There were four soldiers at a crucifixion and five pieces of garments. The seamless tunic was put into the lottery rather than being divided.

Christ of God, Chosen One: Terms referring to His claim to be the Messiah.

Sixth hour: Noon. His crucifixion began at 9:00 A.M. and was over by 3:00 P.M.

Temple veil: The cloth curtain that separated the Holy area of the temple from the most sacred area called the Holy of Holies. It was Jewish belief that God's presence dwelt in the Holy of Holies.

Luke 24:1-12

[1] On the first day of the week, very early in the morning, the women took the spices they had prepared and went to the tomb. [2] They found the stone rolled away from the tomb, [3] but when they entered, they did not find the body of the LORD Jesus. [4] While they were wondering about this, suddenly two men in clothes that gleamed like lightning stood beside them. [5] In their fright the women bowed down with their faces to the ground, but the men said to them, "Why do you look for the living among the dead? [6] He is not here; he has risen! Remember how he told you, while he was still with you in Galilee: [7] 'The Son of Man must be delivered into the hands of sinful men, be crucified and on the third day be raised again.'" [8] Then they remembered his words.

[9] When they came back from the tomb, they told all these things to the Eleven and to all the others. [10] It was Mary Magdalene, Joanna, Mary the mother of James, and the others with them who told this to the apostles. [11] But they did not believe the women, because their words seemed to them like nonsense. [12] Peter, however, got up and ran to the tomb. Bending over, he saw the strips of linen lying by themselves, and he went away, wondering to himself what had happened.

Highlight the main and minor characters.

Where and when does this story take place?

What are the key events, activities, or ideas?

How did the characters respond? Why?

How is Jesus described (by Himself or others, claims made, character traits displayed)?

What values were taught/demonstrated by Jesus?

Beliefs (truths, principles taught or demonstrated by Jesus)

Conclusions (implications, if . . . then)

BACKGROUND

The tomb was sealed with a large stone. In other accounts, the women discussed how to remove the stone.

Other accounts in the Bible record the appearance of angels in the form of men. The dazzling appearance fitted the spiritual beings from the realm of glory and purity.

The eleven disciples were now minus Judas, who had committed suicide following his betrayal of Jesus.

In addition to the twelve disciples that followed Jesus closely, there was also a group of women who had been part of the intimate group of followers. Mary Magdalene, Joanna, and Mary the mother of James were some of this group of women who discovered the empty tomb.

KEY WORDS

The tomb: Belonged to Joseph of Arimathea; carved out of the rock. It was likely close to Jerusalem.

Spices: Used to anoint a body for burial. The burial on Friday evening had been hurried due to the approaching Sabbath. The proper procedure had not taken place.

The two men: The other accounts identify these men as angels.

Son of Man: The title Jesus identified with that meant the One who was coming.

John 3:1-16

[1] Now there was a man of the Pharisees named Nicodemus, a member of the Jewish ruling council. [2] He came to Jesus at night and said, "Rabbi, we know you are a teacher who has come from God. For no one could perform the miraculous signs you are doing if God were not with him."

[3] In reply Jesus declared, "I tell you the truth, no one can see the kingdom of God unless he is born again."

[4] "How can a man be born when he is old?" Nicodemus asked. "Surely he cannot enter a second time into his mother's womb to be born!"

[5] Jesus answered, "I tell you the truth, no one can enter the kingdom of God unless he is born of water and the Spirit. [6] Flesh gives birth to flesh, but the Spirit gives birth to spirit. [7] You should not be surprised at my saying, 'You must be born again.' [8] The wind blows wherever it pleases. You hear its sound, but you cannot tell where it comes from or where it is going. So it is with everyone born of the Spirit."

[9] "How can this be?" Nicodemus asked.

[10] "You are Israel's teacher," said Jesus, "and do you not understand these things? [11] I tell you the truth, we speak of what we know, and we testify to what we have seen, but still you people do not accept our testimony. [12] I have spoken to you of earthly things and you do not believe; how then will you believe if I speak of heavenly things? [13] No one has ever gone into heaven except the one who came from heaven—the Son of Man. [14] Just as Moses lifted up the snake in the desert, so the Son of Man must be lifted up, [15] that everyone who believes in him may have eternal life.

[16] "For God so loved the world that he gave his one and only Son, that whoever believes in him shall not perish but have eternal life."

Highlight the main and minor characters.

Where and when does this story take place?

What are the key events, activities, or ideas?

How did the characters respond? Why?

How is Jesus described (by Himself or others, claims made, character traits displayed)?

What values were taught/demonstrated by Jesus?

Beliefs (truths, principles taught or demonstrated by Jesus)

BACKGROUND

When the Jewish people left captivity in Egypt and were traveling in the desert, they rebelled against God. God judged them by sending a "fiery serpent" among the people resulting in many deaths. When the people confessed their sin, God told Moses to make a brass image of the serpent and place it on a pole in the camp. When those who were bitten looked at the brass serpent, they were restored to health.

KEY WORDS

Pharisee: The most strict and influential of three prominent societies of Judaism at the time of Christ. They were experts in the interpretation of Scripture and considered the religious leaders.

Nicodemus: Held a very prominent position. He was a member of the Sanhedrin, a scribe (a teacher of the law), as well as a Pharisee.

Rabbi: Master or teacher.

Kingdom of God: Used in various ways but always implying "that where God rules."

Son of Man: A phrase used by Jesus to describe Himself. It referred to the One who was coming again to rule the world. It was not as inflammatory as the title of Messiah, yet conveyed both deity and humanity.

APPENDIX

BASIC LAWS OF SPIRITUAL ECONOMICS

1. We have been created to know God but our independence has offended His holy nature, leaving us alienated and spiritually bankrupt.

   Romans 3:23 "For all have sinned and fall short of the glory of God."

   Romans 3:10 "As it is written, 'There is none righteous, not even one.'"

2. The currency of personal merit is debased and worthless to God. No amount of reorganization will deliver us from debt.

   Ephesians 2:8-9 "For it is by grace you have been saved through faith—and this not from yourselves, it is the gift of God—not by works, so that no one can boast."

3. God's love is expressed in Jesus Christ. His death on the cross is the only currency that can adequately satisfy God's holiness and secure our debt in full.

   Romans 5:8 "But God demonstrates his own love for us in this: While we were sinners, Christ died for us."

4. Through declaration of personal, moral bankruptcy and faith in Christ, we can receive deliverance from our debt, initiate a personal relationship with God, and receive the gift of life that is eternal.

   John 5:24 "I tell you the truth, whoever hears my word and believes him who sent me has eternal life and will not be condemned; he has crossed over from death to life."

SPIRITUAL JOURNEY

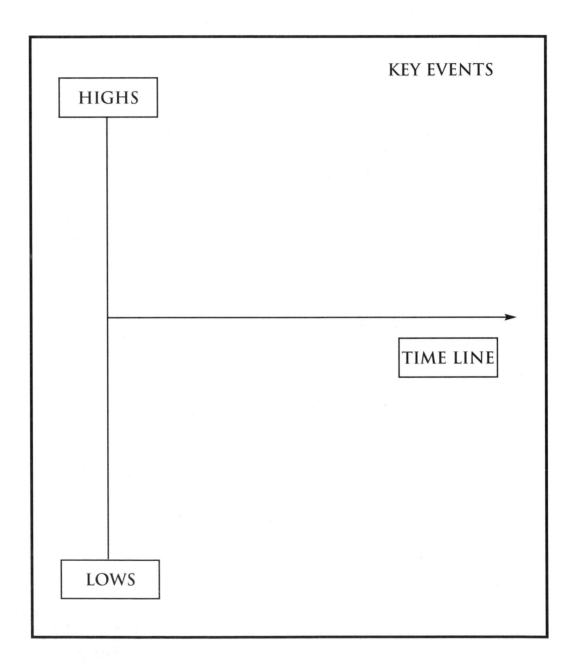

KEY EVENTS

HIGHS

TIME LINE

LOWS

BRIDGE ILLUSTRATION
(© 1969, The Navigators)
Available for sale in tract form from The Navigators
A summary of the gospel
A visual presentation

Draw and share the following presentation using a blank sheet of paper and the Bible. This presentation is most effective after you have gained permission to share a summary of what the Bible teaches regarding becoming a real Christian.

The illustration uses four verses of Scripture, which you should look up and read together. They form the authoritative basis for the principles presented.

The illustration is built around five points or principles:

    1. God's Purpose

        2. Man's Problem

            3. God's Plan

                4. God's Provision

                    5. Man's Prerogative

By memorizing these five points and the four accompanying verses, you can make a clear presentation in a relaxed, conversational manner.

1. GOD'S PURPOSE

The Bible begins by showing us that originally God created man to share His image and an intimate relationship. Man and God were in perfect union. I will let the following line represent this union and fellowship.

However, that union was broken by man's decision to become morally independent from God. That independence is also called disobedience or sin.

Man	God

This sin resulted in alienation or separation from God. The intimacy was gone. Man and God no longer experienced a personal relationship. Man became spiritually dead. That condition has been historically passed down through every generation since Adam.

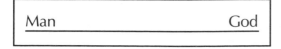

I will highlight that separation by drawing two cliffs with a gulf in between. Man is on one side and God is on the other.

2. MAN'S PROBLEM

The Bible describes man's problem in a statement found in Romans 5:12. Would you read it? I'd like to have you identify a couple of key points.

From that statement, what characterizes all men and women? [Sin]

What does it say is the result of that sin? [Death]

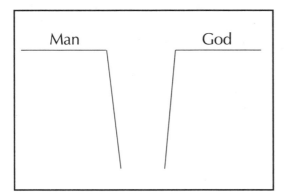

The basic meaning of the word death is separation. Death in its various forms resulted from man's sin. That death is experienced in every area of life: physically, emotionally, socially, psychologically, and spiritually.

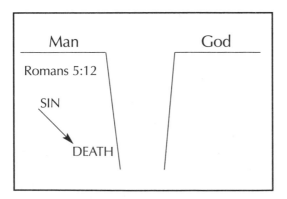

Ultimately, death leads to an eternal separation from God and His purpose.

3. GOD'S PLAN

The Bible also reveals God's plan. Read this statement in John 3:16 and I'll have you highlight some concepts from it.

The Bible reveals a lot about the character of God. What is the characteristic that this statement highlights? [Love] What does this statement say is the result of God's love? [Life!]

Like death, life has various aspects. The Bible teaches that God desires to put life back together in every aspect that was destroyed

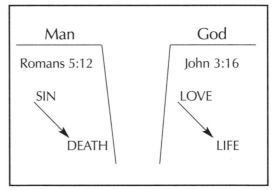

by sin. Ultimately, God desires to give us life that is eternal, life that has no end and restores the union and intimacy that were lost.

4. GOD'S PROVISION

Throughout human history, man has tried to reach God in various ways. Basically it boils down to man attempting to do more good than bad. He hopes that the good works will balance the scale in his favor.

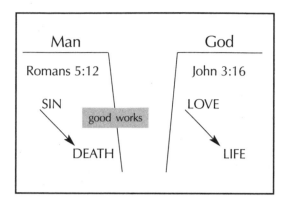

Man's good works are always inadequate to span the gulf created by sin. Self-effort in any form falls short of God's standard of holiness.

God is consistent with both His love and His holiness. His holiness demands that man's sin has to be accounted for and His love demands a response of grace. God's provision for man deals with the sin issue through His grace.

Read the statement in Romans 5:8 and we'll notice how this provision works.

Notice the progression as it follows the illustration: God . . . love . . . us . . . sinners . . . Christ . . . died . . . for us.

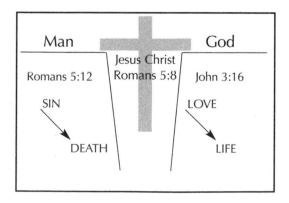

Jesus Christ was God's provision for the problem of man's sin. His death and resurrection provided the bridge that can reunite man with God. It is the only means by which this union can be restored. Jesus said, "I am the way, the truth, and the life. No man comes to the Father but by me."

5. MAN'S PREROGATIVE

One other statement from John 5:24 explains how an individual can cross over the bridge that Christ has provided. After you read it, I want to ask you a couple of questions that highlight the main concepts.

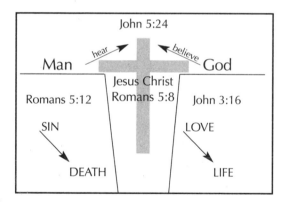

From that statement, what is Christ offering man?

1. Eternal life
2. No judgment
3. Passage from death to life

What then is necessary to receive this offer?

1. Hear my word
2. Believe in him who sent me

The term "belief" in the Bible means more than acknowledgment of facts or information. The words "believe in" mean to trust in, commit to, rely upon, or receive.

A person becomes a child of God and is reunited to a personal relationship with Him when he or she comes to a personal commitment of faith in Jesus Christ. God's provision has been extended to us. It is a gift. As a gift, we cannot work for it—only receive it.

Does this illustration make sense to you?

Have you ever heard these concepts before?

What questions do you have?

• Where would you place yourself along the diagram?

• Would you be willing by faith to accept Christ as your bridge to God right now?

You can express this step of faith in a simple prayer in which you need to tell God:

1. I recognize that I am separate from You as a result of my sin.

2. I recognize that Christ was Your provision for me . . . to die for my sin.

3. I want to accept by faith Your gift of forgiveness through Christ.

4. I thank You for Your forgiveness and accepting me as part of Your family.

First John 5:11-12 gives a birth certificate for those who receive Christ. It is critical to read and explain the significance of these verses.

BRIDGE ILLUSTRATION

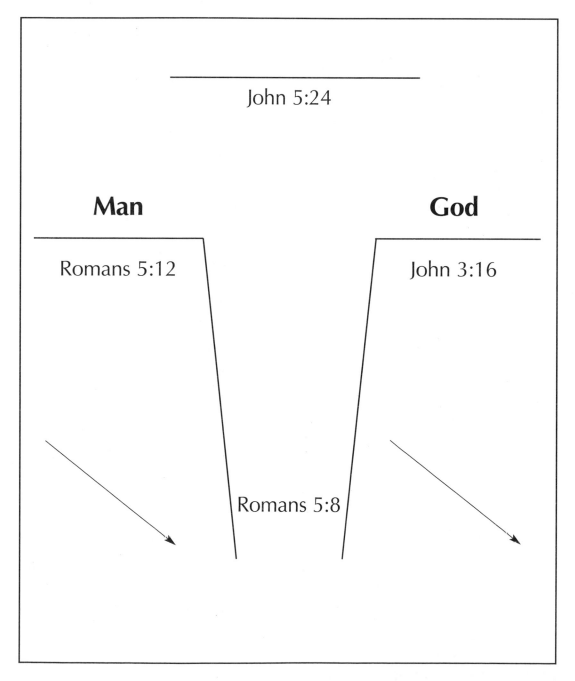

John 5:24

Man   **God**

Romans 5:12   John 3:16

Romans 5:8

CDM Church Discipleship Ministry

A MINISTRY OF THE NAVIGATORS

CDM is a ministry of The Navigators that focuses on helping churches become more intentional in discipleship and outreach. CDM staff help pastors and church leaders develop an effective and personalized approach to accomplishing the Great Commission.

Through a nationwide network of staff, CDM works alongside the local church to build a strong structure for disciplemaking—one that is intentional. Six critical areas are core to an Intentional Disciplemaking Church:

- Mission

- Spiritual Maturity

- Outreach

- Leadership

- Small Groups

- Life-To-Life

CDM offers seminars, materials, and coaching in these six areas for those interested in becoming an Intentional Disciplemaking Church. See our web page for further information on how CDM can help you.

www.navigators.org/cdm

or call our CDM Office at (719) 598-1212
or write to P.O. Box 6000, Colorado Springs, CO 80934

Discipleship Resources from
Church Discipleship Ministry (CDM)
and NavPress

☐ *Opening the Door*
- A user-friendly, seeker-oriented tool for helping people explore the Gospel message
- A tool kit full of tips on being an effective facilitator and recruiting new seekers
- Twenty Discovery Guides each using selected passages from the Gospel of Luke
- Each Discovery Guide can be photocopied and used for every new group or individual you intend to reach.
- Each Discovery Guide contains only one Scripture reading and eight questions, allowing discussions to be completed in less than an hour over lunch or coffee.

Available from NavPress 1-800-366-7788

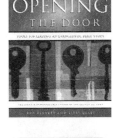

☐ *Intentional Disciplemaking: Cultivating Spiritual Maturity in the Local Church*
A disciplemaking church significantly impacts its members and its environment. But how does a church make disciples? Disciples don't just happen. They're developed through intentional planning and the effort of a community of believers. While many churches want to produce solid Christian disciples, they are not intentional about making it happen. They don't have a plan. Here's help for churches that want to make disciples—on purpose.

Available from NavPress 1-800-366-7788

The resources listed below are available from the Church Discipleship Ministry of The Navigators, at 1-719-598-1212 x2446:

☐ *Mission Master Plan (MMP)*
This vision-building working resource will help your church develop its own foundational elements of Purpose, Vision, Core Values, and Philosophy of Ministry. It also helps you create the bridge to your future through identifying: Critical Success Factors, Goals, Action Steps, and Vital Communication.

☐ *Leadership Assessment and Development (LAAD)*
This leadership consultation tool will assist your church leadership team in assessing how they are preparing leaders. It looks at your leadership profile and your development process and helps you assess and correct missing steps.

☐ *Authentic Evangelism Seminar (AES)*
This one-day training seminar helps a church develop the vision and strategy for intentional outreach. In addition to helping individuals become more confident in sharing their faith, it helps mobilize the whole church body toward using their gifting in reaching out to a broken world.

☐ *Discipling Others Seminar (New from CDM)*
This one-day seminar prepares disciples to disciple others. DOS will launch new disciplers into authentic discipling using either mentoring or small groups. This interactive seminar covers: The Vision for Making Disciples, Creating a Disciplemaking Environment, and Ministering Life-To-Life.